THE FORMATION OF PROF

Becoming a lawyer is about much more than acquiring knowledge and technique. As law students learn the law and acquire some basic skills, they are also inevitably forming a deep sense of themselves in their new roles as lawyers. That sense of self—the student's nascent professional identity—needs to take a particular form if the students are to fulfil the public purposes of lawyers and find deep meaning and satisfaction in their work. In this book, Professors Patrick Longan, Daisy Floyd, and Timothy Floyd combine what they have learned in many years of teaching and research concerning the lawyer's professional identity with lessons derived from legal ethics, moral psychology, and moral philosophy. They describe in depth the six virtues that every lawyer needs as part of his or her professional identity, and they explore both the obstacles to acquiring and deploying those virtues and strategies for overcoming those impediments. The result is a straightforward guide for law students on how to cultivate a professional identity that will allow them to make a meaningful difference in the lives of others and to flourish as individuals.

Patrick Emery Longan is William Augustus Bootle Chair in Ethics and Professionalism in the Practice of Law at the Mercer University School of Law and Director of the Mercer Center for Legal Ethics and Professionalism. Professor Longan is a graduate of Washington University, the University of Sussex, and the University of Chicago Law School. Professor Longan's work relating to professionalism and professional identity has been recognized by his receipt of the 2005 National Award for Innovation and Excellence in Teaching Professionalism and by the Mercer Law School's receipt of the 2014 E. Smythe Gambrell Professionalism Award.

Daisy Hurst Floyd is University Professor of Law and Ethical Formation at Mercer University School of Law, where she served as Dean from 2004 to 2010 and again from 2014 to 2017. Her teaching and research interests include Ethics, Legal Education, Civil Procedure, and Evidence. She has a particular interest in the ways in which higher education shapes students' ethical development and in cross-disciplinary collaborations. Professor Floyd was named a Carnegie Scholar by The Carnegie Foundation for the Advancement of Teaching in 2001 in support of her research on the development of professional identity among American law students. She received her BA and MA from Emory University and her JD from the University of Georgia School of Law.

Timothy W. Floyd is Tommy Malone Distinguished Chair in Trial Advocacy and Director of Experiential Education at Mercer University School of Law. In addition to supervising clinical and externship programs, he has taught courses in legal ethics, criminal law, civil procedure, legal skills, law and religion, and human rights. He has published two books and is the author of numerous articles in the area of legal ethics, law and religion, criminal law, and the death penalty. While teaching at several law schools in his career, he has represented persons facing the death penalty and worked to insure access to justice for all in civil cases. He received his BA and MA from Emory University and his JD from the University of Georgia.

THE FORMATION OF PROFESSIONAL IDENTITY

The Path from Student to Lawyer

PATRICK EMERY LONGAN, DAISY HURST FLOYD, AND TIMOTHY W. FLOYD

Routledge
Taylor & Francis Group

LONDON AND NEW YORK

First published 2020
by Routledge
2 Park Square, Milton Park, Abingdon, Oxon OX14 4RN

and by Routledge
52 Vanderbilt Avenue, New York, NY 10017

Routledge is an imprint of the Taylor & Francis Group, an informa business

British Library Cataloguing-in-Publication Data
A catalogue record for this book is available from the British Library

Library of Congress Cataloging-in-Publication Data
A catalog record has been requested for this book

ISBN: 978-1-138-65168-5 (hbk)
ISBN: 978-1-138-65169-2 (pbk)
ISBN: 978-1-315-62468-6 (ebk)

Typeset in Joanna MT Std
by codeMantra

This book is dedicated to our students — past, present, and future.

CONTENTS

PREFACE

This book grew out of our experiences teaching a required first-year course on professionalism and professional identity at the Mercer University School of Law. We hope that students and teachers alike will benefit from the lessons that we have learned along the way and that we have tried to convey in this book.

In 1996, the Professionalism Committee of the American Bar Association Section on Legal Education and Admissions to the Bar, under the leadership of former ABA President Reece Smith, recommended that law schools devote more class time to lawyer professionalism, beyond discussion of the Model Rules of Professional Conduct. The Committee called particularly for a course for first-year law students and predicted that most law schools would find such a dramatic change to the curriculum to be difficult.

The Mercer faculty responded to this call with a plan to add a professionalism course to the required first-year curriculum. Even in its planning stages, it was clear that the course would be about what has come to be known as professional identity. Professor Jack Sammons, the original mastermind behind the course, wrote in an internal planning document, "the course will not be so much about what a student should do as it will be about who a student is to become." Because there was no similar course being taught at any law school, planning took several years.

The "Legal Profession" course is what emerged from that process, and it became a part of Mercer's required first-year curriculum in the spring of 2004. The course was not an immediate success. There was no blueprint for how to expand legal ethics instruction beyond the rules of conduct, and students did not always react well to the early versions of the course. Nonetheless, Mercer's faculty was extremely patient. The first year is the most prized real estate in the law school curriculum, but the faculty allowed the course to evolve and mature. We kept trying different things. Some worked. Other did not. But every year, we gained more and more valuable hands-on experience with how issues of professional identity play out in the law school classroom.

While we were learning from our trial and error approach, a professional identity movement in legal education gathered steam. The Carnegie Foundation for the Advancement of Teaching conducted a thorough study of American legal education, culminating in the publication of Educating Lawyers: Preparation for the Profession of Law in 2007. Drawing upon the work of its lead author, philosopher William Sullivan, the Carnegie Report emphasized that law schools can and should do more to cultivate the professional identities of their students. The concept of professional identity has helped many of us in legal education to see that law school is about more than what lawyers should think and do; legal education is also, as Jack Sammons had noted years before, about who our students are becoming.

Neil Hamilton and Jerry Organ at the University of St. Thomas Law School Holloran Center took up the call of Educating Lawyers and have continued and advanced the conversation on professional identity. Larry Krieger at Florida State published ground-breaking work (some in collaboration with Ken Sheldon at Missouri) on the relationships between professional identity and well-being. Mercer's Jack Sammons and Mark Jones, and North Dakota's Michael McGinnis, produced scholarship that infused the professional identity movement with the insights of Aristotle's virtue ethics. Clark Cunningham at Georgia State, through the National Institute for Teaching Ethics and Professionalism, brought many of us together every year to explore these issues. Among the many things that Clark did for all of us was that he introduced us to Muriel "Mickey" Bebeau from the University of Minnesota, and Mickey brought moral psychology into our discussions. More recently, Dr.'s Richard and Sylvia Cruess shared with us the benefit of their ground-breaking work on professional identity formation in medical schools.

Today we believe that our course is a success. We have learned from our own experience what to expect from students when they first encounter the notion of professional identity formation and how to, as Neil Hamilton would say, "meet them where they are." We learned from our colleagues around the country to structure the course with its deep intellectual underpinnings in place. We have put those ingredients together into what we believe to be a recipe for successful professional identity instruction.

In this book, we seek to share what we have learned. It is our hope that the book will be useful in a variety of ways. We realize that few law teachers have the luxury we have of a three-credit course devoted solely to professional identity formation. We therefore deliberately made the book as concise as possible, in the hope that it might be suitable as a supplement for a course on professional responsibility or useful in an externship or clinical setting. Some schools offer short courses on professionalism, and the book certainly would be helpful there. But regardless of how it is used, we hope that the book will play a part in helping this generation of law students understand what professional identity is, why it is crucial to make an internal commitment to developing the right kind of professional identity, and how to go about implementing that commitment.

ACKNOWLEDGEMENTS

This book is the result of many years of learning from countless others who generously shared with us their experience, insights, and wisdom. We are especially indebted to Patti Aleeva, Muriel Bebeau, John Berry, Susan Brooks, Dick Cruess, Sylvia Cruess, Clark Cunningham, Ron Ellington, Jim Elliott, Natt Gantt, David Grenardo, Benjamin Grimes, Neil Hamilton, Mark Jones, Kendall Kerew, Larry Krieger, Sally Lockwood, Ben Madison, Michael McGinnis, Jerry Organ, Jack Sammons, Barry Schwartz, Kenneth Sharpe, Marjorie Silver, Roy Sobelson, Bill Sullivan, and Judith Wegner.

We thank Shandi Kennedy and Gretchen Longan, each of whom read and commented on the manuscript. We also deeply appreciate Dr. Mary Wilder, Professor Emeritus of English at Mercer University, who read the manuscript, red pen in hand, and eventually gave us a passing grade.

1

INTRODUCTION AND OVERVIEW

LAW SCHOOL AND THE TRADITIONAL VALUES OF THE LEGAL PROFESSION

Law school changes you. You learn things that lawyers need to know. You learn how to do some of the things that lawyers need to know how to do. But the changes you are experiencing are more fundamental and subtler than just the acquisition of knowledge and skill. You are also, intentionally or not, absorbing lessons about the professional values that are supposed to guide the deployment of your new-found knowledge and skill.

This part of your education goes by various names. The Carnegie Foundation's study of legal education used an analogy to apprenticeship and described law school as involving three apprenticeships (Sullivan et al. 2007). The first two apprenticeships concern knowledge and skill, respectively. Education about professional values is the so-called "third apprenticeship." Others use a different and more general term, "socialization," to refer to the process by which individuals learn and internalize the values of a particular group (Cruess and Cruess 2016). Whether you call the process apprenticeship or socialization, the fact is that law school seeks to instill in you the traditional values of the legal profession.

That notion might at first rankle you. You came to law school as an adult with well-developed personal values. You may be one of the many law students who have rebellious and nonconformist streaks and bridle at the notion of absorbing any "traditional" values. These concerns are common among law students, but we will be making the case that these understandable concerns are misplaced. The professional values we are talking about will not displace your personal values. Rather, your personal and the professional values will need to be integrated. And the traditional values of the legal profession do not forbid all forms of rebellion and nonconformity. Far from it, lawyers are expected to challenge authority and the status quo. But one thing you need to accept at this early stage is that by choosing to enter the legal profession you have submitted yourself, to some extent, to the authority of the profession. There is plenty of room for individuality in the law, but there are certain non-negotiable values that lawyers must have in order to do the jobs that society demands of them. Part of the good news that comes with that, as you will see, is that the internalization and deployment of these values will make it more likely that you will find deep meaning in your work.

This book is about teaching you what those values are, convincing you to incorporate them into your sense of self as a lawyer, and helping you to live up to them when you become a lawyer.

LAW SCHOOLS AND THE TRANSMISSION OF VALUES

Law school historically has not been as good about transmitting the values of the profession as it has been about teaching knowledge and, to a lesser extent, skill.

Socialization by fear of discipline

The accreditation standards for U.S. law schools mandate that every school must require all of its students "to satisfactorily complete … one course of at least two credit hours that includes substantial instruction in rules of professional conduct…" (American Bar Association Section of Legal Education and Admission to the Bar 2018, 16). Fulfillment of this Standard usually comes in the form of a required upper-level course (often called Professional Responsibility or "PR") that focuses on the American Bar Association Model Rules of Professional Conduct. Every state has rules of conduct that are based, to a greater or lesser degree, on the Model Rules. Study of the Model Rules provides some guidance to students about the values of the profession and motivates conduct that lives up to these values primarily by the fear of discipline such as disbarment.

As a way of transmitting the values of the legal profession and motivating you to live up to them, the PR course is important but incomplete. Not all of the values of the profession are reflected in the rules. For example, as you will see, civility is a core value of the legal profession. Yet there is no "civility rule" in the Model Rules. Furthermore, many kinds of misconduct are difficult to detect and therefore difficult to punish. For example, another core value is fidelity to the law, and one of the Model Rules requires lawyers not to assist witnesses in testifying falsely. But how would the bar ever detect such coaching in the privacy of the lawyer's office? Finally, deploying the values of the profession in complex circumstances requires much more than knowledge of the "do's and don'ts." Often the value-laden decision for the lawyer is about what you *should* do, among multiple permissible actions. Knowing the rules of conduct and the possible consequences of violating them is important, but the socialization process requires more.

Socialization by aspiration: the modern professionalism movement

More recently, some law schools have exhorted students to "aim higher" than the rules and aspire to act with "professionalism." This movement, of which we have been a part, broadens the conception of a lawyer's professional responsibilities in important ways. In 1986, the American Bar Association Commission on Professionalism issued a report, a "Blueprint for the Rekindling of Lawyer Professionalism." That report resulted from calls from Chief Justice Warren Burger and bar leaders for the American Bar Association (ABA) to study professionalism in light of widespread perception that the bar "might be moving away from the principles of professionalism…" (American Bar Association Commission on Professionalism 1986, v). The ABA Blueprint was the beginning of the modern professionalism movement, which has now spawned numerous codes, creeds and statements of professionalism as well as more than a dozen state commissions on professionalism and mandatory professionalism continuing legal education in a handful of states. Dozens of law schools now have programs or courses that concern professionalism in some way. Some of these courses are explicitly designed to expose first-year students to the values of the profession and begin the socialization process.

Professionalism training is a useful supplement to learning about the rules of conduct because it conveys the values of the profession more broadly that the PR course does. One of the early proponents of professionalism, Chief Justice Harold Clarke of the Supreme Court of Georgia, once famously wrote that "ethics is a minimum standard which is *required* of all lawyers while professionalism is a higher standard *expected* of all lawyers" (Clarke 1989, 173). Such expectations do not fit comfortably into a regulatory framework such as a rule of conduct but can find useful expression in an aspirational statement on professionalism.

One shortcoming of professionalism training is motivation. The underlying theme of the professionalism movement is to inspire students and lawyers, to convince them that they *should* conduct themselves in particular ways, even when no rule requires them to do so and they need not fear any punishment. That is why we call this type of training "socialization by aspiration." Some students respond to this type of appeal, but many resist. Part of the problem is that, frankly, professionalism teaching can sound a little preachy. The teacher quotes from the holy writ of the professionalism creed, or the civility guidelines, or some other such pronouncement, and exhorts the students to live up to the Word and sin no more. Maybe it is generational, but our experience has been that most law students do not respond to preaching. You are in the midst of rigorous training to be critical thinkers, and you are understandably skeptical of received wisdom. It is also important to realize that most of you are in your mid-twenties. We offer no scientific studies to back this up, but our experience has been that many of our students are in the early stages of evolving from a self-centered orientation to an other-centered view of the world. Our students almost never have a true appreciation for what it means to be a fiduciary. You may not yet have such an appreciation. Telling you that one of the core values of the legal profession is fidelity to the client, which may involve self-sacrifice, may therefore strike a discordant note.

Another problem with professionalism teaching is that it does not provide any guidance on how to turn noble aspirations into action in particular situations. Being able to recite professionalism verses does not solve real-world problems. It is like telling a pianist about all the beautiful notes but providing no guidance about which notes to play in which order. The beautiful notes are no practical good at concert time.

Courses and programs on professionalism have been an important step in the right direction of a more comprehensive process of socializing law students into the values of the profession. However, now that the shortcomings in such training are clear, another approach is needed. That is where "professional identity" comes in.

A third way: the cultivation of professional identity

We advocate a third way of socializing you into the values of the profession: the acquisition and cultivation of a "professional identity" that internalizes the values of the profession and thereby disposes you to practice in accordance with them. Professional identity formation, as a means of socialization into a profession, is not original with us, nor is it new. But we offer our own specifics about the components of the right kind of professional identity for lawyers and, based upon our experience in teaching legal ethics and professionalism, how you can best begin the process of professional identity formation and continue that process after you graduate.

An identity, as we define it, is a deep sense of self in a particular role. Whether or not you have thought about it this way, you had several such identities when you started law school. You may have had identities as a son or daughter, as a sibling, as a friend, as a student, or as an employee. In each such role, you could describe what kind of person you are or hope to be, such as the kind of friend who can be relied upon in times of need. As you go through life, you will form other identities. If you have not done so already, you likely will form identities as a spouse and maybe as a parent. Probably without realizing it, you have formed an identity as a law student. You might try the exercise of completing the sentence, "I am the kind of law student who ____." Your overall sense of self evolves and grows in complexity as you undertake and integrate the various roles you play in your life.

Professional identity is a piece of this evolving sense of self. Once you are in practice, you will have a deep sense of yourself *as a lawyer*. You will be able to fill in the blanks of the sentence, "I am the kind of lawyer who ____." Your previous identities—as a friend, spouse, etc.—will not work as your identity as a lawyer. Put simply, you have never been a lawyer and thus could not come to law school with any deep sense of yourself in this new role.

Your development of a professional identity as a lawyer does not mean the disappearance of your other identities. As we have said, we all live our lives every day with multiple senses of ourselves in our different roles. As you navigate the various roles you have or acquire in life, you may act simultaneously as a lawyer *and* a spouse, as a lawyer *and* a person of faith, or as a lawyer *and* a parent, and so on. You will never be *just* a lawyer. Although you are not *replacing* your existing identities, you will need to find a way to *integrate* them. For your own psychological health, your senses of yourself in your different roles should not conflict with each other in fundamental ways—they should cohere in integrated, mutually enforcing ways. It is unhealthy to be "one person at home" and "another person at the office." Psychological research makes it clear that such a lack of integrity (in the sense of "wholeness") among your various roles is a formula for distress and anxiety.

It is crucial at the outset to see two things. First, professional identity formation is inevitable. You will form a sense of yourself as a lawyer, but it can happen by design or by drift. You can be active or passive about what kind of lawyer you become. Second, the content of your professional identity is not pre-determined. Not all lawyers see themselves as lawyers in the same way. There are lawyers who would describe their senses of self in their roles as lawyers by saying, "I am the kind of lawyer who wins at all costs," or "I am the kind of lawyer who is a pit bull in trial or deposition," or "I am the kind of lawyer who makes the most money." Those are professional identities. Other lawyers might define themselves as "the kind of lawyer who is faithful to my clients" or "the kind of lawyer who serves the public interest." Those, too, are professional identities. Within the limits of what might get you disbarred, you have the power to shape your own professional identity. But not all professional identities are created equal.

We contend that you should be intentional about the formation of your professional identity and that your professional identity should take a particular form, one that incorporates the traditional core values of the legal profession. There are two prongs to our argument. The prongs happily converge. The first is that, with the right kind of professional identity, you are more likely to serve your clients well and fulfill the public purposes of lawyers. Your work will matter to others. The other is that with such a professional identity you are more likely to find your work meaningful and thereby to derive a sense of well-being and satisfaction. Your work will matter to you. We turn now to an overview of what we mean by "the right kind of professional identity."

THE SIX VIRTUES OF THE PROFESSIONAL LAWYER

Identity is a matter of character. If you take a moment to define your identity in a role that you already have, you will discover that almost certainly you define yourself not by how you behave in particular situations but rather by character traits that help you fulfill that role. For example, you probably would say that your identity as a friend includes being loyal. As a son or daughter, you might say that part of your deep sense of self in that role is that you are respectful. Your identity as a spouse probably includes being attentive to the feelings of your spouse.

In classical terms, character traits that form a healthy identity are *virtues*. They are capacities or dispositions that bring you closer to an ideal. Without the capacity to be loyal, you would be less of a friend. Because you are respectful, you are a better son or daughter. And so on. We will have more to say about virtue and professional identity for lawyers—particularly about the insights of modern "virtue ethics"—but for now it suffices if you see that the "right kind of professional identity" is one that incorporates whatever virtues are needed for the particular role of being a professional lawyer.

There is remarkable consensus in the legal profession about the virtues necessary to be the kind of lawyer who serves clients well and helps to fulfill the public purposes of the profession. The "traditional values" of the profession, stated broadly, are not controversial (although application of those values to particular situations may spark intense disagreement). As we have noted, the ABA Model Rules are a partial expression of those values, and the various codes and creeds that emerged from the professionalism movement contain more expansive and detailed expressions of those values. These documents reflect substantial consistency about what the profession values in a lawyer.

From our study of the Model Rules and the various professional codes and creeds, we have concluded that there are six virtues that should become parts of your professional identity. We will discuss each of these six virtues in detail in later chapters. For now, we will briefly explain what each virtue includes and why it matters, both to individuals and more broadly to society. Note particularly how we present the virtues. We name them, but we then express them in the first person, as a lawyer's sense of self. We phrase them in this way to help you see the virtues as components of professional identity.

The virtue of competence

"I am an excellent lawyer, one who has the knowledge, skill, diligence and judgment to assist my clients."

Competence matters. It is obvious why individual clients need competent lawyers. Clients seek legal help in times of conflict and stress, when they face problems that they cannot solve on their own. At best, an incompetent lawyer will do the client no good. At worst, an incompetent lawyer will make matters worse. Good office lawyers help clients avoid disputes, but incompetent ones fail to prevent disputes or, worse, foment them. Good courtroom lawyers provide effective and efficient representation for clients. Incompetent ones can cost a client his or her money, freedom, or life.

Lawyer competence is also crucial for broader social purposes. Every avoidable conflict that an office lawyer does not foresee or prevent leaves the doors open for later litigation. The public bears much of the cost. Courtroom lawyers who do not know what they are doing multiply and delay proceedings, with the result that the courts are unnecessarily congested. Others who need resolution of their disputes must wait. Every unjust result allowed by an incompetent lawyer also has a public cost. Such results, if they become known, undermine faith in the judicial process and invite people to seek other, possibly more destructive, ways of resolving their disputes.

It is important to note here at the outset that "competence" for a lawyer is a broader and more complex concept than you might think. In Chapter 3, we will explore in depth the various components of what we mean by lawyer competence.

The virtue of fidelity to the client

> "I am a lawyer who fulfills my duties of utmost good faith and devotion to my client, and I do not permit my personal interests or the interests of others to interfere with those duties."

Fidelity to the client matters to individual clients. Clients often come to lawyers at time of great vulnerability, and lawyers are in positions to take advantage. A lawyer who lacks the virtue of fidelity to the client might charge the client too much, use the client's confidential information to the lawyer's advantage, or sell out the client to benefit the lawyer or another client. Often clients are not in a position to observe such acts of disloyalty. A lawyer who does not have the virtue of fidelity to the client can harm clients and sometimes get away with doing so.

Fidelity to the client is also crucial for lawyers to serve their broader purposes. Lawyers cannot help to avoid disputes or secure fair and efficient resolution of disputes if clients do not trust them enough to consult them. If someone is sick but does not trust doctors, he may ignore his illness or self-medicate and thereby create public health dangers. Someone who has a legal problem but does not trust lawyers—because she believes that she cannot trust lawyers to be faithful—may either ignore the problem or represent herself. Either option is likely to impose public costs, either by an unnecessary dispute or the grinding inefficiencies of pro se representation in court.

The virtue of fidelity to the law

> "I am a lawyer who is faithful to and upholds the law and the institutions of the law."

The virtue of fidelity to the law serves client interests and helps to fulfill the public purposes of lawyers. Most clients want to comply with the law. Lawyers, as experts in the boundaries of the law, serve those clients well when they dissuade the clients from illegal activity. Even clients more disposed to law-breaking are well served by lawyers who not only refuse to help them but also advise them of the consequences of the proposed course of action.

Fidelity to the law and its institutions is critical for fulfillment of the public purposes of the legal profession. Society has an interest in seeing that its laws are obeyed. Lawyers serve the rule of law, and promote compliance with the law, when they persuade clients not to engage in illegal activities and refuse to assist. Fidelity to the law is also crucial in judicial proceedings. There are opportunities for lawyers to cheat for their clients. The lawyer might, for example, hide evidence, suborn perjury, or bribe the judge. But cheating is a form of corruption, and a system that is perceived to be corrupt will not be seen as legitimate. Our judicial process depends mostly on voluntary obedience to its dictates, and that voluntary obedience erodes once the process is perceived as illegitimate. The peaceful resolution of disputes through the judicial system is possible, therefore, only if lawyers exercise the virtue of fidelity to the law and its institutions and refuse to cheat.

The virtue of public spiritedness

I am a lawyer who practices in a spirit of public service. I seek to ensure access to justice and to regulate the legal profession for the benefit of the public. I do my share to represent unpopular people and causes, and I seek to improve the law."

We need lawyers who see themselves as public servants. At the individual level, there are many people in our society who cannot afford lawyers even in times of desperate need. Every time a lawyer represents a client pro bono in resisting eviction, or obtaining public benefits, or securing a writ of habeas corpus, or in any number of other contexts, that lawyer is rendering a great service to that individual. Individual clients who face public scorn or prejudice against them also benefit when a lawyer with the virtue of public service has the courage to step in to protect them.

Society more broadly needs such lawyers. Proceedings that would otherwise involve pro se parties are fairer and more efficient when lawyers get involved. The parties and the public will accept the results of such proceedings more readily because the results are more legitimate. Regulation of the legal profession in ways that prevent misconduct, or otherwise promote the public interest rather than the profession's interest, protects every client and potential client. When a lawyer steps forward to protect an unpopular client or cause, the public benefits (whether it realizes it or not) because the protection of the worst preserves the protection of all. Improvement of the law benefits everyone.

The virtue of civility

"I am a lawyer who is civil to everyone with whom I come in contact as a lawyer. I am courteous, cooperative, and honest, and I do not engage in abusive tactics."

Clients sometimes think they want lawyers who are rude and otherwise uncivil. The clients respond to advertisements in which lawyers promise to be nasty and uncooperative with opposing parties. Lawyers who internalize the virtue of civility serve those clients well by not succumbing to such understandable temptations of the clients or the selfish desire to attract clients by promising uncivil conduct. Incivility is expensive. It drives up the costs of litigation, both financial and psychological, and it feeds on itself. Incivility begets more incivility. It prevents compromise or reconciliation. Clients may not realize it at first, but they are ill-served by lawyers who are rude, uncooperative, dishonest, and abusive. The lawyer who displays civility better serves the long-term interests of individual clients.

Civility is essential if our dispute resolution systems are to perform efficiently. Our judicial system is utterly dependent upon the cooperation of counsel. Although there are rules of procedure that one can invoke for virtually every contingency, the system would fail of its own weight if everything had to be done "by the book." Such conduct would hobble the ability of the judicial system to render just or efficient results. There are not enough judges in the country to referee every dispute among contentious counsel. Every minute of judicial time devoted to petty disputes that flow from discourtesy, lack of cooperation, lack of trust, or abusive litigation tactics is time away from deciding the merits of other disputes. It is also likely that rampant incivility may drive out of the profession individuals who have low tolerance for such conduct, with the result that the profession could enter a spiral of more and more inefficient and destructive incivility.

The "master virtue" of practical wisdom

"I am a lawyer who cultivates the practical wisdom that I need in order to deploy my other virtues, both personal and professional, in particular situations in the right amounts, in the right way, and for the right reasons."

As a lawyer, you will not act in the abstract. You will have to take action in particular circumstances. We hope you will approach each such occasion with a deep sense of your own personal identity and of yourself as a lawyer who is competent, faithful to your clients, faithful to the law, public-spirited, and civil. But particular circumstances may bring these parts of your personal and professional identities into tension with each other. You might best serve your client by engaging in a discourteous cross-examination of an untruthful opposing party. You may need to interpret a document request from an opposing party knowing that, under one interpretation, you will have to turn over a "smoking gun" to the opposition. Or perhaps you could take advantage of another lawyer's mistake and obtain a result that, as a matter of your personal values, you may consider to be fundamentally unfair. And so on. To make matters worse, you might have to make such decisions under conditions of high stakes and irreducible uncertainty.

Practical wisdom is the "master virtue" that enables you to chart a course in such difficult moments of professional practice. It presupposes that you have internalized the other five virtues and recognized their importance for individual clients and for society more generally. Your job in these moments is the hardest and most satisfying job you will ever have as a lawyer: to decide on what the right thing is to do, to make sure you are choosing that action for the right reasons, and to implement that action in the right way. By definition, because practical wisdom requires the possession of the other virtues, practical wisdom serves both individual and societal interests.

THE CONDITIONS NECESSARY FOR PROFESSIONAL IDENTITY DEVELOPMENT

We said earlier in this chapter that the purposes of this book are to teach you the traditional values of the legal profession, to convince you to incorporate those values into your sense of self as a lawyer, and to help you to live up to those values when you become a lawyer. In other words, for you to possess and deploy the right kind of professional identity, you must be *sensitized* to what that means and what may impede you, you must be *motivated* to make the effort to do so, and you must have the skill to *reason* to and *implement* a decision in particular circumstances. We did not choose these goals, or this terminology, idly. We have borrowed them from moral psychology, particularly the Four

Component Model of Morality (FCM) (Bebeau and Monson 2008). We are not psychologists, but we believe that the FCM provides powerful insights into the conditions necessary for the cultivation of your professional identity and a useful structure for understanding the process. The rest of this book is organized around those insights. Here we provide a short summary of the FCM.

The FCM posits that there are four distinct but interactive components to moral action. All must be present for an individual to act morally in a particular circumstance. The four components are moral sensitivity, moral motivation, moral reasoning, and moral implementation.

Moral *sensitivity* involves a deep awareness of various factors at play in a situation, including recognition that there is an issue that must be dealt with; the likely reactions and feelings of others; knowledge of alternative courses of action, including the possible consequences and their effects on multiple parties; the ability to see things from the perspectives of other individuals and groups and from legal and institutional perspectives; and knowledge of the regulations, codes, and norms of one's profession and when they apply. In terms specifically of your professional identity development as a lawyer, sensitivity includes an ability to detect when a situation calls for one or more of the six virtues and recognition of any obstacles to their deployment.

Moral *reasoning* refers to formulating and evaluating possible solutions to the moral issue. This step in the process requires reasoning through the possible choices and potential consequences to determine which are ethically sound. Moral reasoning is a skill that will enable you in particular circumstances to think through the applicability of each of the six virtues and to evaluate how proposed courses of action implicate the virtues.

Moral *motivation* has to do with the importance given to moral values in competition with other values. At a macro level, the lawyer must find motivation to undertake the effort to develop the right kind of professional identity. In a specific situation, a lawyer might be tempted by values such as self-interest not to be faithful to a client or to the lawyer's responsibilities to the court or opposing lawyers and parties. The lawyer must find a reason to act in accordance with the six virtues. We will explore this question of motivation in detail in the next chapter.

Moral *implementation* focuses on whether a person has sufficient pertinacity, toughness, ego strength, judgment, and courage to implement a course of action that emerges from his or her moral reasoning. A person may be morally sensitive, may make good moral judgments, and may place a high priority on moral values, but if the person wilts under pressure, or is easily distracted or discouraged, then moral failure occurs because of deficiency in this component. As part of a lawyer's professional identity, one can view moral implementation as an advanced and complex form of competence, one that often requires the master virtue of practical wisdom.

We believe the FCM is a helpful way to structure your thinking on professional identity, and the organization of this book reflects that. Chapter 2 addresses the issue of *motivation* and discusses why you should make the internalized commitment to develop your professional identity in accordance with the six traditional values of the profession. Chapters 3 through 8 focus on each of the six lawyer virtues in isolation, with the purposes of *sensitizing* at greater depth regarding what each virtue means, why it matters, and what obstacles there are to its deployment, and each of these chapters also provides some guidance on how to *implement* a commitment to deployment of that virtue. In particular, Chapter 8 on practical wisdom takes the questions of *reasoning* and *implementation* to a deeper level of complexity and explores how to deploy the traditional virtues of the legal profession in circumstances of conflict and uncertainty. We conclude with Chapter 9, which confronts the issue of the enduring importance of the six virtues as the legal profession changes in the decades to come.

CONCLUSION

You almost certainly made the decision to come to law school because you intend to make the practice of law your vocation. Author Frederick Buechner once wrote that vocation is where "the world's deep need" meets your "deep gladness" (Buechner 1973, 118). The world has a deep need for lawyers who choose to internalize a professional identity that enables them to deploy the six virtues. The good news for you, and the subject of the next chapter, is why such a choice is likely to lead to your "deep gladness." Remember that one of the four necessary conditions for professional identity acquisition and deployment is motivation. As you will see, the motive for you to work on the right kind of professional development is that this is a path to satisfaction in your chosen profession and well-being in your life.

DISCUSSION QUESTIONS AND PROBLEMS

1   This chapter begins with the statement, "Law school changes you." Reflect upon the ways in which, for good or ill, law school is changing you and your sense of self. Think about whether those changes will support or hinder "the right kind of professional identity" as we have described it in this chapter. Also reflect upon whether the changes have been the result of a conscious choice or whether they seem have occurred without you deciding upon them.

2   You may have never consulted a lawyer, but you almost certainly have interacted with physicians who were caring for you or for members of your family. Describe the virtues that, you believe, are the necessary virtues for a physician to have in order for the physician to fulfill the purposes of the medical profession. Describe an experience with a physician who exemplified one or more of these virtues and an experience with a physician who did not.

3   Pick another role you have in life, as a friend, sibling, or spouse, for example. Reflect upon and articulate your sense of yourself in that role. Describe your identity in that role as the possession and deployment of one or more virtues. For example, complete the sentence, "I am the kind of spouse who ____." Identify as many of the relevant virtues for that role as possible.

4   Identify a lawyer (real of fictional) whom you admire. Using the structure and language of this chapter, explain why you admire the lawyer. What virtues does the lawyer possess and deploy, and how do those virtues relate to the six virtues we described in this chapter?

5   We have described for you the six virtues that need to be part of your professional identity if you are to be the kind of lawyer who fulfills the purposes of the profession. Those professional virtues will need to be integrated with your personal values, or ethos—the principles that already guide your conduct. Articulate your personal ethos and explain how you plan to integrate your personal values with the six virtues. Identify any conflicts or obstacles that you expect to encounter in the integration of your personal and professional values.

REFERENCE LIST AND SUGGESTED READINGS

American Bar Association. 2018. *Model Rules of Professional Conduct*. www.americanbar.org/groups/professional_responsibility/publications/model_rules_of_professional_conduct/model_rules_of_professional_conduct_table_of_contents/.

American Bar Association Commission on Professionalism. 1986. "…In the Spirit of Public Service," A Blueprint for the Rekindling of Lawyer Professionalism. *Federal Rules Decisions* 112: 243.

American Bar Association Section of Legal Education and Admission to the Bar. 2018. *Standards and Rules of Procedure for Approved Law Schools*. www.americanbar.org/groups/legal_education/resources/standards/.

American Bar Association Section of Legal Education and Admission to the Bar. 1996. *Teaching and Learning Professionalism, Report of the Professionalism Committee*. Chicago: American Bar Association.

American Bar Association Standing Committee on Professionalism. 2013. *Essential Qualities of the Professional Lawyer*, ed. Paul A. Haskins. Chicago: ABA Publishing.

Bebeau, Muriel J., Stephen J. Thoma, and Clark D. Cunningham. 2017. Educational Programs for Professional Identity Formation: The Role of Social Science Research. *Mercer Law Review* 68:591.

Bebeau, Muriel J., and Verna E. Monson. 2008. Guided by Theory, Grounded in Evidence: A Way Forward for Professional Ethics Education. *Handbook of Moral and Character Education*, ed. Larry Nucci, Darcia Narvaez, and Tobias Krettenauer. New York: Routledge.

Bell, Derrick. 2002. *Ethical Ambition: Living a Life of Meaning and Worth*. New York: Bloomsbury.

Brooks, David. 2015. *The Road to Character*. New York: Random House.

Buechner, Frederick. 1973. *Wishful Thinking: A Seeker's ABC*. San Francisco: Harper & Row.

Clarke, Harold G. 1989. Professionalism: Repaying the Debt. *Georgia Bar Journal* 25:170.

Cunningham, Clark D. 2015. Learning Professional Responsibility. *Building on Best Practices: Transforming Legal Education in a Changing World*, ed. Deborah Maranville, Lisa Radtke Bliss, Carolyn Wilkes Kaas, and Antoinette Sedillo Lopez. New Providence: Matthew Bender.

Cruess, Richard L., and Sylvia R. Cruess. 2016. Professionalism and Professional Identity Formation: The Cognitive Base. *Teaching Medical Professionalism: Supporting the Development of a Professional Identity*, ed. Richard L. Cruess, Sylvia R. Cruess, and Yvonne Steinert. Cambridge: Cambridge University Press.

Cruess, Sylvia R., and Richard L. Cruess. 2017. From Teaching Professionalism to Supporting Professional Identity Formation: Lessons from Medicine. *Mercer Law Review* 68:665.

Gantt, Larry O. II, and Benjamin V. Madison III. 2015. Teaching the Newly Essential Knowledge, Skills, and Values in a Changing World. *Building on Best Practices: Transforming Legal Education in a Changing World*, ed. Deborah Maranville, Lisa Radtke Bliss, Carolyn Wilkes Kaas, and Antoinette Sedillo Lopez. New Providence: Matthew Bender.

Jaeger-Fine, Toni. 2019. *Becoming a Lawyer: Discovering and Defining Your Professional Persona*. St. Paul: West Academic Publishing.

Kronman, Anthony T. 1993. *The Lost Lawyer: Failing Ideals of the Legal Profession*. Cambridge: Belknap Press.

Linder, Douglas O., and Nancy Levit. 2014. *The Good Lawyer: Seeking Quality in the Practice of Law*. New York: Oxford University Press.

Longan, Patrick E. 2009. Teaching Professionalism. *Mercer Law Review* 60:659.

Sammons, Jack L. 2003. Cheater!: The Central Moral Admonition of Legal Ethics, Games, Lusory Attitudes, Internal Perspectives, and Justice. *Idaho Law Review* 39:273.

Sullivan, William M. 2005. *Work and Integrity: The Crisis and Promise of Professionalism in America*. San Francisco: Jossey-Bass.

Sullivan, William M., Anne Colby, Judith Welch Wegner, Lloyd Bond, and Lee S. Shulman. 2007. *Educating Lawyers: Preparation for the Profession of Law*. San Francisco: Jossey-Bass.

2

MOTIVATION AND PROFESSIONAL IDENTITY

INTRODUCTION

We saw at the end of Chapter 1 that one of the conditions necessary for you to acquire and cultivate the right kind of professional identity is that you must be motivated to do so. The process requires you to learn what the profession expects of you and about all the forces you will encounter that will make fulfilling those expectations difficult. You have to learn how to make and implement decisions that implement the six virtues. You have to practice at it. Sometimes you will fail. Then you will try again. It can be frustrating. Sometimes exercise of the virtues will mean that you must act contrary to your economic self-interest. You may find that hard to do, especially at first. The virtues might require you to act in ways that cause you to lose friends. That, too, can be difficult. Yet the expectations of the profession do not yield.

Why should you bother? Our argument is simple: it is in your personal interest to do so, for the sake of your own well-being and sense of fulfillment as a lawyer. It is a self-serving decision to cultivate a professional identity that incorporates the six virtues. We find support for this proposition in insights that come from a field of psychology known as Self-Determination Theory, or SDT, and empirical evidence that supports the theory. We also find support in a branch of moral philosophy known as virtue ethics. We will explore those subjects in this chapter. However, before we use these insights to commence an argument about the relationship between professional identity and happiness as a lawyer, we need to start by alerting you to current concerns about the well-being of members of the legal profession. We believe that those concerns will make our prescription—professional identity formation as a path to a sense of well-being—all the more attractive.

WELL-BEING AMONG LAWYERS AND LAW STUDENTS

Bar associations are focusing intensive attention on issues of attorney and law student well-being. In 2017, the American Bar Association National Task Force on Lawyer Well-Being issued its report, in which it defined well-being "as a continuous process whereby lawyers seek to thrive in each of the following areas: emotional health, occupational pursuits, creative or intellectual endeavors, sense of spirituality or greater purpose in life, physical health, and social connections with others" (American Bar Association National Task Force on Lawyer Well-Being 2018, 9).

The profession is focusing attention on well-being because of concerns that a significant minority of lawyers and law students are not thriving. There are some troubling statistics. In 2016, the ABA Commission on Lawyer Assistance Programs and the Hazelden Betty Ford Foundation conducted a study of mental health and substance abuse disorders among lawyers (Krill, Johnson and Alpert 2016). The study found that, of the 13,000 practicing lawyers who responded to the survey, 20.6% screened positive for hazardous, harmful or potentially alcohol-dependent drinking (compared to 11.8% of other highly educated members of the work force). Of the lawyers surveyed, 28% experienced mild or higher levels of depression. Alarmingly, the study found that lawyers in the first ten years of practice and those working in private firms experienced the highest rates of problem drinking and depression.

The results were also disturbing in a 2016 survey of law student well-being (Organ, Jaffe and Bender 2016). Of those surveyed, 17% experienced some level of depression, 14% experienced severe anxiety, and 23% had mild or moderate anxiety. Six percent reported serious suicidal thoughts in the past year. The students were asked about binge drinking, and 43% reported binge drinking at least once in the prior two weeks while 22% reported binge drinking two or more times during that period. Twenty-five percent were considered to be at sufficient risk for alcoholism that further screening was recommended.

It is important for you to realize that a substantial percentage of disciplinary proceedings and malpractice claims against lawyers involve substance use, depression, or both. This is not surprising. Alcohol use and depression are strongly associated with cognitive impairments that interfere with the ability to solve problems and plan for the future, both of which are essential for good lawyering.

We report these statistics not to scare or depress you but rather to alert you that there are troubling patterns in the profession. Too many lawyers and law students are not thriving. We also seek to encourage you. It is possible, using SDT and virtue ethics, to identify conditions that will maximize your chances of well-being in the profession. The insights from positive psychology and moral philosophy will help you see the connection between a professional identity that incorporates the six virtues and your own well-being. Our hope is that seeing those connections will help convince you to make the commitment to cultivation of such a professional identity and help you thrive as a lawyer.

SELF-DETERMINATION THEORY, PROFESSIONAL IDENTITY, AND WELL-BEING

The needs, values, and motivations of SDT

SDT is a branch of positive psychology that yields powerful and testable insights into the relationship between professional identity and well-being (Ryan and Deci 2017). Thriving, according to SDT, includes positive aspects of human experience, including positive mood and affect, life satisfaction, a sense of purpose, and effective performance. Well-being is associated with the fulfillment of fundamental psychological needs and with particular values and motivations.

SDT posits that humans have three basic psychological needs that are essential for well-being. They are *autonomy, competence,* and *relatedness*. One's actions are *autonomous* if they are perceived as self-directed and volitional, rather than controlled by others. *Competence* is the sense of mastery and of feeling able to operate effectively in important aspects of life. The third fundamental need, *relatedness*, includes a sense of belonging.

In addition to the three needs, SDT also relates well-being to different kinds of values. SDT holds that four *intrinsic values* support the satisfaction of the three fundamental needs. Those values are *self-understanding/growth, intimacy with others, helping others,* and *being in/building community.* In contrast, SDT predicts that certain *extrinsic values* will be associated with a lack of well-being. Those *extrinsic values* are *high earnings, status, appearance,* and *influence over others.*

Finally, SDT associates thriving with *intrinsic motivations* and *identified motivations* as opposed to *extrinsic motivations.* One is *intrinsically* motivated to engage in activities that are enjoyable for their own sake rather than as a means to some other end. You have done things because of intrinsic motivation. You may have derived intrinsic joy from music, dance, basketball, chess, or any number of other activities you have done for their own sake. You have also probably acted from an *identified* motivation, which is one that leads you to devote time and energy to something deeply valued. A person motivated in this way might willingly do things that bring no intrinsic reward because those things are meaningful ways of furthering a fundamental purpose. For a simple example, someone who is devoted to preserving the environment might spend time picking up trash next to a highway. Picking up trash is not intrinsically enjoyable, but it serves a purpose that is important to that person. In contrast, one is *extrinsically* motivated to engage in activities that are instrumental, in that they lead to consequences one desires. Everyone is so motivated to some extent. Perhaps you worked an extra job to buy a new car. The work might have been dull and, in and of itself, meaningless, but it was a means of getting the money to pay for the pleasure of that new-car smell.

SDT and professional identity formation

The formation of a professional identity that incorporates the six virtues will feed the three basic psychological needs of autonomy, competence and relatedness and also will support the values and motivations associated with thriving.

Start with the virtue of competence. By definition, a professional identity that internalizes a commitment to excellence and ongoing improvement serves the fundamental psychological need for a sense of *competence.* Such a commitment increases the chances that you will feel mastery as a lawyer. The professional virtue of competence also supports the psychological need for *autonomy.* If you have gained the necessary knowledge, developed the requisite skill, and married those aspects of competence to diligence, you will be prepared to handle what the practice of law throws your way without usually having to look outside yourself. You will be, and feel, more autonomous. An ongoing commitment to improvement also aligns with the value of *growth,* while it also makes it more likely that you will be able to *help others.*

Cultivation of fidelity to the client as an internalized virtue serves the psychological need for *relatedness.* Relatedness includes having a sense of significance to others. Clients often seek out lawyers at times of severe distress and vulnerability. The lawyer then becomes the voice for the clients and the clients' guide through the confusing and frightening processes of the law. The devotion and self-lessness that are part of fidelity to the client justifiably creates a sense that the lawyer is significant to the client. It is also a source of *intimacy* with the client and of a sense of *helping others.*

The virtue of fidelity to the law helps to fulfill the need for *relatedness* and the value of *being in/building community*. When we talk about lawyers' higher duties to the law and the courts, we often describe ourselves as "officers of the court." Lawyers serve together, in relationship with each other and the court. We are part of a community, a corps of justice in a sense. We also refer to fellow lawyers as our "brothers and sisters at the bar." That phrase also captures a sense of community in our role "at the bar," where we exercise our fidelity to the law and the courts.

The virtue of public-spiritedness helps to satisfy our need for *relatedness* and relates to all of the intrinsic values of SDT. When we render pro bono service, or regulate ourselves for the benefit of others, or represent unpopular causes or clients, we *serve others*. Such actions connect us to those on whose behalf we act. Undertaking a pro bono matter that is outside our usual expertise requires us to understand our limitations and experience *growth*. Even if the work itself is not intrinsically rewarding, it may result from an *identified motivation* to ensure that the poor receive representation regardless of their ability to pay for it. When we represent a pro bono client or an unpopular client or cause, we are creating the *intimacy* of the attorney-client relationship and *helping others*. Service to the public is by its very nature an act of *community*. By rendering that service through organizations such as a bar association, a lawyer is in and helps build the organization as a *community*.

The virtue of civility also feeds the need for *relatedness* and the values of *self-understanding/growth* and of *being in/building community*. Civility requires us to be courteous, cooperative and honest with adversaries. Acquiring a disposition to civility demands *self-understanding* to recognize the causes of the temptations not to be civil and *growth* as we learn to rise above those temptations. When as lawyers we do not allow the acrimony of clients or the stakes of a particular matter to affect our personal relationships, we *build a community* of professionals and occupy our place in that community.

The virtue of practical wisdom is a complex and extremely rewarding form of *competence*. As an iterative process of learning by doing, it will be associated with *growth*, and it is employed to *help others*. It too, like the other virtues, relates to SDT's needs, values and motivations.

The point is that, if the insights of SDT are correct, you are much more likely to thrive if you cultivate a professional identity that incorporates the six virtues. The right kind of professional identity formation will help to fulfill the basic psychological needs for autonomy, competence and relatedness, and the six virtues each relate to one or more of those needs and one or more of the intrinsic values that SDT associates with well-being. Professional identity formation is also strongly tied to intrinsic motivation, another correlate of well-being. The good news is that there is significant empirical evidence that these predictions of SDT about lawyers and their professional identities are correct.

Empirical evidence relating to professional identity and well-being

Professors Lawrence Krieger (a lawyer) and Kennon Sheldon (a psychologist) used SDT and conducted an extensive survey of practicing lawyers to try to assess what makes lawyers happy (Krieger and Sheldon 2015). They asked samples of lawyers in four states to complete a lengthy survey about the lawyers' subjective senses of well-being, symptoms of depression, alcohol use, law school experiences, current working circumstances, personal life choices, and other factors. They eventually generated a sample size of over 7,800 respondents. Their hypotheses were that indicators of well-being in the legal profession would be strongly correlated with the needs, values, and motivations set forth in SDT.

Those hypotheses proved to be correct. Krieger and Sheldon found strong associations between attorneys' well-being and measurements of the lawyers' senses of autonomy, competence, and relatedness. These measures were much more powerfully correlated with well-being than with external factors such as law school class rank and income. You may find it particularly interesting that the Krieger and Sheldon study of lawyers found that class rank ultimately had very little to do with attorneys' well-being, and law review membership showed zero correlation with well-being.

Krieger and Sheldon had previously conducted two studies of law students that showed a decline in measures of well-being during law school (Sheldon and Krieger 2004). They found that, as SDT predicts, those effects were correlated with changes related to values. The studies showed marked shifts among law students away from intrinsic values such as helping others toward external values such as rewards (high grades) or status (academic rank in class).

Krieger's and Sheldon's studies also provide empirical evidence for SDT's prediction about lawyer well-being and motivation. Their study of lawyers showed a strong correlation between internal motivations and well-being. Their studies of students found significant declines in the students' well-being after they entered law school and showed that, as the students' well-being declined, their motivations for becoming lawyers had changed. The students' motivations had changed from intrinsic or identified (for the enjoyment of the work or for work with meaning) to extrinsic (such as recognition for high grades and status from rank in class).

These studies are strong evidence, as SDT predicts, that your personal well-being will be strongly associated with needs, values, and motivations that in turn are closely related to the six virtues of the professional lawyer.

The Krieger and Sheldon studies are not the only empirical evidence that associates the six virtues with SDT's requirements for thriving. Recall that a basic psychological need is competence, or mastery. SDT posits that you will have a stronger sense of well-being—you are more likely to thrive—if you have what it takes to be an effective lawyer. So, what does it take? It turns out that much of "what it takes" to be an effective lawyer flows from the acquisition of the six virtues.

Empirical evidence for this conclusion comes from Educating Tomorrow's Lawyers (ETL), an initiative of the Institute for the Advancement of the American Legal System, an independent national research center based at the University of Denver. In 2014, ETL undertook its "Foundations for Practice" project and sought to find out, among other things, what practicing lawyers think are the most important "foundations" that lawyers need to be competent right away, in the short term (Educating Tomorrow's Lawyers 2016). ETL defined "foundations" as the skills, competencies, characteristics, abilities, behaviors, capacities, knowledge, traits, qualities, and all other similar factors that a lawyer might need. ETL came up with a list of 147 such foundations and surveyed over 24,000 lawyers in 37 states about them. The survey asked the lawyers to put the various foundations into "buckets," one of which was for foundations that a lawyer needs in the short term.

The results show that lawyers recognize that, for the most part, what is needed for early success as a lawyer is a set of character traits that would be part of a professional identity that incorporates the six virtues. Among the top 20 foundations of success as a lawyer are "integrity and trustworthiness," "treating others with courtesy and respect," "a strong work ethic," "a strong moral compass," "common sense" and the "ability to write and speak professionally." The relationship between these "foundations" and the six virtues of competence, fidelity to client, fidelity to law, public-spiritedness, civility, and practical wisdom should be apparent. The bottom line is that cultivation of the six virtues will make you a better lawyer and, because SDT teaches us that a sense of competence or mastery is so important to your sense of well-being, the development of the right kind of professional identity will help you thrive.

Professor Neil Hamilton and Verna Monson reached the same conclusion (Hamilton and Monson 2011). They used a definition of professionalism that overlaps substantially with the six virtues we have identified, and they examined the relationship between professionalism as they defined it and studies of effectiveness of lawyers. They concluded that professionalism contributed significantly to high effectiveness. In our terms, an internalized professional identity that includes the six virtues will be highly correlated with effectiveness, which in turn is associated with fulfilment of the psychological need for competence and personal well-being.

Insights from SDT help you understand why it is in your personal interest to acquire and cultivate the right kind of professional identity. But there is more to the argument than psychology. A branch of moral philosophy known as virtue ethics provides further support for this conclusion.

VIRTUE ETHICS

Virtue ethics is a normative theory, which means that is about how one *ought* to act. There are other normative theories of ethics. *Consequentialism* would say that one ought to act in whatever way achieves the best result, or consequence. *Deontological ethics* is not so result-oriented but instead is duty-based; one's actions are judged according to whether they comply with applicable rules.

Virtue ethics is different. It dates back to Aristotle and focuses not on consequences or duties but rather on character. It posits that right action will emerge from the cultivation and deployment of deeply ingrained character traits, or virtues. Virtue ethics supposes that there is a goal to which you might aspire. For example, you might aspire to be a good soldier. There are virtues that will enable you to move closer to the ideal of a soldier. The virtue of bravery would be on that list. At the same time, there are vices, which are character traits that would move you in the opposite direction. A vice for a soldier would be cowardice. Or think of it in terms that are closer to home. You surely aspire to be a good law student. Among the virtues that will move you closer to the ideal of a good law student would be diligence, resilience, and open-mindedness. Vices would include slothfulness, inattentiveness, and rigidity.

In Chapter 1, we described professional identity as a matter of character, and we labeled the particular character traits necessary to be a good lawyer as "virtues." Now you may begin to see why we chose that particular nomenclature.

The connection of virtue ethics to the goal of being a good lawyer is this. We have listed six virtues (expressed as components of professional identity) that, if you cultivate and deploy them, will move you closer to the ideal of a professional lawyer. You could name some vices that take you in the other direction. Among those that probably come readily to mind are ineptitude, dishonesty, and selfishness. Professional identity formation, seen as the cultivation of the lawyerly virtue, nests comfortably in the framework of virtue ethics.

Virtue ethics will also help you understand more complex questions. It recognizes that the right action is not always a simple matter of identifying the necessary virtue and deploying it. For one thing, there can be too much of a good thing. A good soldier, for example, might not deploy the unalloyed virtue of courage in every circumstance of battle. Too much courage becomes foolhardiness. At the other extreme, a soldier who deployed too little courage in particular circumstances would be displaying timidity. The virtuous soldier is courageous but not foolhardy or timid. The soldier finds the right amount of the virtue necessary to the circumstances.

In the context of lawyering, too much fidelity to the client could cause a lawyer to lie and cheat. Too little would lead to self-dealing. Too little civility would lead to unnecessarily contentious and expensive proceedings. Too much civility might sacrifice a client's legitimate interests. And so on. The lawyer must find the appropriate intermediate ground for the particular situation.

Another complication with which virtue ethics helps is that, in complex circumstances, virtues can conflict with one another. If a friend asks you if he looks good in a particularly ugly suit, do you deploy the virtue of truth or the virtue of compassion, or what combination of the two? Such situations lead virtue ethics to emphasize the necessity of the master virtue of practical wisdom, which will enable you to chart a course that deploys the right virtues in the right combination. As a lawyer, practical wisdom is what will enable you to decide how to balance the other five virtues when they conflict with one another. A fellow lawyer might ask for an extension of time that would cause some prejudice to your client. Do you give priority to civility or fidelity to the client? Or perhaps an extra bit of diligence, which is part of competence, might yield some benefit to your client but at some (perhaps excessive) cost to your client. Is it right to be faithful to the client and minimize cost or to go the extra mile in service to competence? You get the idea.

Virtues ethics is also a helpful lens through which to see the personal rewards of professional identity formation. As far back as Aristotle, virtue ethics was about happiness, or "human flourishing." Aristotle believed that the path to a life well lived was the development and exercise of virtue. But a more contemporary and vivid way of understanding the connection between your flourishing and your professional identity as a lawyer is to have a basic understanding of the work of the modern philosopher Alasdair MacIntyre.

MacIntyre explored virtue and its rewards through the concept of a "practice." His definition of a "practice" is dense and may appear at first to be obscure. Here it is:

> By a 'practice' I am going to mean any coherent and complex form of socially established cooperative human activity through which goods internal to that form of activity are realised in the course of trying to achieve those standards of excellence which are appropriate to, and partially definitive of, that form of activity, with the result that human powers to achieve excellence, and human conceptions of the ends and goods involved, are systematically extended.
>
> (MacIntyre 2007, 175)

MacIntyre gives examples. The games of football and chess are practices, each with its own internal standards of what it means to be an excellent player. The fields of architecture, physics, chemistry, biology, and history are practices, as are the arts of painting and music. Again, each has defined within itself what it means to be a good architect or biologist, etc.

To bring this closer to home for you, think of being a law student as a "practice." It has internal standards of excellence that are appropriate to the endeavor. Good law students are punctual, diligent, prepared, honest, cooperative, courageous, respectful, and resilient (among other things). You no doubt have discovered that those standards are different from the standards of being an excellent high school or college student. So, ever since you started law school, you have been engaged in a practice as defined by MacIntyre without even knowing it.

Law is certainly a practice within MacIntyre's definition. It is a "coherent and complex form of socially established cooperative human activity." The practice of law has internal standards of excellence that are "appropriate to" the practice. These are the character traits that define what it means to be a good lawyer. They are the six virtues of competence, fidelity to the client, fidelity to the law, public-spiritedness, civility, and practical wisdom.

The connection between a "practice" and your motivation to cultivate the right kind of professional identity is this. MacIntyre notes that one can engage in a practice, like the practice of law, for different types of rewards. MacIntyre distinguishes between "external goods" and "internal goods." External goods are easy to explain and envisage. An external good is something separate and apart from the practice except that participating in the practice is a way of acquiring the external good. Typical examples are money, fame, and power. Some lawyers get rich, famous, and powerful as a result of practicing law. Their toil has yielded external goods. External goods are finite, and one must compete to achieve more of them, at the expense of others who compete for them.

Again, just to make it vivid, think about the "practice" of being a law student. There are external goods for that practice. You can name them. They include good grades, rank in class, law review membership, and job prospects. Notice again that external goods are finite and competitive. If rank in class is an external good, then only 50% of the class can be in the top half of the class. Law school is not Lake Wobegone, where all the children are above average.

The concept of "internal goods" is subtler. MacIntyre explains: "Someone who achieves excellence in a practice, who plays chess or football well or who carries through an enquiry in physics or an experimental mode in painting with success, characteristically enjoys his achievement *and his activity in achieving*" (MacIntyre 2007, 184) (emphasis added). In other words, engaging in a practice in accordance with the practice's standards of excellence brings its own internal rewards, apart from anything gained by the activity. Like what you felt from whatever activity in the past has brought you joy just from the act of engaging in and excelling at it, practicing law the right way can be its own reward.

Anthony Kronman, former dean of the Yale Law School, has expressed the point in this way, in answering the question why being a lawyer is a worthwhile endeavor (Kronman 1987). Kronman writes about a conception of law practice

> *that sees the value of what lawyers do, for the lawyers themselves, not so much in the fruits of their work as in the excellences of character their work requires them to develop and permits them to display. Conceived in this way, the value of law practice is clearly something intrinsic to it...*
>
> *(Kronman 1987, 846)*

In other words, practicing law in accordance with the highest standards of the profession brings its own, intrinsic rewards regardless of whether you gain money, fame or power. Kronman also describes his point this way: "...law practice both requires and tends to encourage certain dispositional attitudes or traits of character... a practicing lawyer not only possesses a set of distinctive skills but is likely to be a particular sort of person as well" (Kronman 1987, 846). Being that person—being the professional lawyer who acts in accordance with the highest standards of the profession—is itself an internal good.

Be careful to realize that, according to virtue ethics as described by MacIntyre, the "internal goods" of the practice of law are only available as a result of practicing according to the standards of excellence, which we have defined to be the six virtues. If you cheat, for example by over-billing a client, or by hiding evidence, you deprive yourself of the internal, intrinsic rewards of displaying fidelity to the client or fidelity to the law. You cheat yourself. You are not, and cannot perceive yourself to be, the "particular sort of person" (as described by Kronman) who has earned the internal goods of the practice. Also, you should see that internal goods are not finite and are not competitive. Every lawyer can achieve them simultaneously. Just because I achieve internal goods of the practice by deploying the six virtues does not mean that it is any harder for you to do so or that the internal rewards will be any less abundant for you.

Think back again to the "practice" of being a law student. MacIntyre's theory of internal goods would tell you that by deploying the standards of excellence of the practice—by being punctual, diligent, prepared, honest, cooperative, courageous, helpful, respectful, and resilient—you will reap internal rewards from the act of being that kind of law student. If you cheat, you deprive yourself of those rewards. And there is no "rank in class" with respect to those rewards. Every student can obtain them.

This brief exposure to virtue ethics is intended to help you understand why you should make the effort to cultivate the right kind of professional identity. Our hope is that it assists you in recognizing and appreciating the promise of internal rewards that will be yours if you practice in accordance with the six virtues.

CONVERGENCE BETWEEN SDT AND VIRTUE ETHICS

We have used insights from SDT and from virtue ethics to try to convince you to undertake the effort to form a professional identity that includes the six virtues. Happily, there is a convergence between the lessons of positive psychology and the lessons of moral philosophy. Notice the connection between MacIntyre's "external goods" and SDT's concepts of "extrinsic values" and "external motivation." Extrinsic values in SDT track MacIntyre's examples of "external goods:" money, fame, and power. An extrinsic motivation in SDT is instrumental, in that its purpose is to lead to desirable consequences. One may be extrinsically motivated to practice law for reasons that have nothing to do with law except insofar as law is one of the ways, perhaps among many ways, to obtain what you desire. Those desires to MacIntyre are external goods.

SDT also posits that acting from *intrinsic* motivations is associated with well-being. You are intrinsically motivated to do something because of the satisfaction that comes from the act of doing it, not as a means to an end. In virtue ethics terms, a lawyer who appreciates the internal goods of practicing law in accordance with the practice's standards of excellence—in accordance with the six virtues—will obtain those goods by the act of acquiring, cultivating, and deploying a professional identity that incorporates those standards. The rewards flow from the work itself and are therefore intrinsic to the work.

CONCLUSION

In this chapter, we have made the case that it is in your interest to develop the right kind of professional identity. Using the tools of SDT and virtue ethics, you may navigate among your needs, values, and motivations to achieve well-being by the acquisition, cultivation and deployment of a professional identity that incorporates the six virtues. That is why you should undertake the effort—for your own good. In the next six chapters, we will explore each of the six virtues in detail, with the purposes of sensitizing you to what each means at a deeper level and to the barriers you will find in practice. We will also along the way begin to equip you to implement the commitment that this chapter has attempted to convince you to make.

DISCUSSION QUESTIONS AND PROBLEMS

1   Much of this chapter concerns the differences among three types of motivations, intrinsic, identified, and extrinsic. Consider the definitions of those types of motivations and reflect on what activities you engage in as a result of each. What do you do simply because you enjoy the activity? What do you do that is not enjoyable but that furthers a fundamental purpose or belief? What do you do just as a means to some other end?

2   Think about "being a law student" as a "practice" as defined by MacIntyre. The text suggests some virtues that would be parts of the standards of excellence that would define the practice. Do you agree that those virtues are part of what it means to be a good law student? What other virtues would you include on the list? To the extent that you exhibit any of the listed virtues, do you believe that you have gained any "internal goods" from the practice of being a law student?

3   Consider MacIntyre's definition of a practice and reflect upon what other "practices" you may have been a part of. Define the virtues of those practices and think about the extent to which you exhibited them and the extent to which you gained "internal goods" from the practices.

4   MacIntyre teaches us that if you cheat in a practice—if you fail to live up to the standards of excellence that define the practice—that you will cheat yourself out of the internal goods of the practice. Have you ever "cheated" while participating in something you would describe as a practice? If so, on reflection did you cheat yourself of the internal goods of the practice?

5   Consider the question of financial success as a lawyer. Some lawyers and some law students would say that they "do it for the money." The pursuit of money is not necessarily a bad thing. We all need some base level of material comfort. But beyond that level, the desire to make a lot money might come from extrinsic motivation for status, or it might come from an identified motivation, such as provision for a child's education. What have you observed about the well-being of people who seem to be motivated by financial success? Does it matter in your opinion whether those motivations for financial success would fit SDT's definition of identified motivation vs. its definition of extrinsic motivation?

6   You read in this chapter about the current concern in the profession for the well-being of lawyers and law students. Reflect on what you have observed in law school about the well-being of your classmates. Have you observed conduct that is detrimental to well-being or that reflects dysfunction? If a new law student came to you and asked for advice about how to "thrive" in law school, what advice would you give?

7   Krieger and Sheldon's studies of law students showed a decline in well-being in the first year and a shift in motivation toward extrinsic values and the extrinsic rewards of law school such as high grades and law review. Do you sense a decline in your sense of well-being since entering law school? If so, in light of what you learned in this chapter, to what would you attribute that decline? Have your values or motivations changed from intrinsic to extrinsic? If so, why would that be? What can you do about it?

REFERENCE LIST AND SUGGESTED READINGS

American Bar Association National Task Force on Lawyer Well-Being. 2018. *The Path to Lawyer Well-Being: Practical Recommendations for Positive Change, the Report from the National Task Force on Lawyer Well-Being.* http://lawyerwellbeing.net/wp-content/uploads/2017/11/Lawyer-Wellbeing-Report.pdf.

Aristotle. 2014. *Nichomachean Ethics.* Translated by C.D.C. Reeve. Indianapolis: Hackett Publishing.

Educating Tomorrow's Lawyers. 2016. *The Whole Lawyer and the Character Quotient.* https://iaals.du.edu/sites/default/files/documents/publications/foundations_for_practice_whole_lawyer_character_quotient.pdf.

Hamilton, Neil W. 2013. Law Firm Competency Models & Student Professional Success: Building on a Foundation of Professional Formation/Professionalism. *University of St. Thomas Law Journal* 11:6.

Hamilton, Neil W. 2015. *Roadmap: The Law Student's Guide to Preparing and Implementing a Successful Plan for Meaningful Employment.* Chicago: ABA Publishing.

Hamilton, Neil, and Verna Monson. 2011. The Positive Empirical Relationship of Professionalism to Effectiveness in the Practice of Law. *Georgetown Journal of Legal Ethics* 24:137.

Jones, Mark L. 2017. Developing Practical Wisdom in the Legal Profession and Beyond. *Mercer Law Review* 68:833.

Krieger, Lawrence S. 2005. The Inseparability of Professionalism and Personal Satisfaction: Perspectives on Values, Integrity and Happiness. *Clinical Law Review* 11:425.

Krieger, Lawrence S. 2011. The Most Ethical of People, the Least Ethical of People: Proposing Self-Determination Theory to Measure Professional Character Formation. *University of St. Thomas Law Journal* 8:168.

Krieger, Lawrence S., and Kennon M. Sheldon. 2015. What Makes Lawyers Happy? A Data-Driven Prescription to Redefine Professional Success. *George Washington Law Review* 83:554.

Krill, Patrick R., Ryan Johnson, and Linda Alpert. 2016. The Prevalence of Substance Use and Other Mental Health Concerns Among American Attorneys. *Journal of Addiction Medicine* 10:46.

Kronman, Anthony T. 1987. Living in the Law. *University of Chicago Law Review* 54:835.

Levit, Nancy, and Douglas O. Linder. 2012. *The Happy Lawyer.* New York: Oxford University Press.

MacIntyre, Alasdair. 2007. *After Virtue.* 3rd ed. Notre Dame: University of Notre Dame Press.

McGinnis, Michael S. 2013. Virtue and Advice: Socratic Perspectives on Lawyer Independence and Moral Counseling of Clients. *Texas A & M Law Review* 1:1.

McGinnis, Michael S. 2011. Virtue Ethics, Earnestness, and the Deciding Lawyer: Human Flourishing in a Legal Community. *North Dakota Law Review* 87:19.

Organ, Jerome M., David B. Jaffe, and Katherine Bender. 2016. Suffering in Silence: The Survey of Law Student Well-Being and the Reluctance of Law Students to Seek Help for Substance Use and Mental Health Concerns. *Journal of Legal Education* 66:116.

Robbennolt, Jennifer K., and Jean R. Sternlight. 2012. *Psychology for Lawyers.* Chicago: American Bar Association.

Ryan, Richard M., and Edward L. Deci. 2017. *Self-Determination Theory: Basic Psychological Needs in Motivation, Development and Wellness.* New York: The Guilford Press.

Schwartz, Barry, and Kenneth E. Sharpe. 2006. Practical Wisdom Meets Positive Psychology. *Journal of Happiness Studies* 7:377.

Seligman, Martin E.P. 2011. *Flourish: A Visionary New Understanding of Happiness and Well-Being.* New York: Simon & Schuster.

Sheldon, Kennon M., and Lawrence S. Krieger. 2004. Does Legal Education Have Undermining Effects on Law Students? Evaluating Changes in Motivation, Values, and Well-Being. *Behavioral Sciences and the Law* 22:261.

Silver, Marjorie A. 2016. Work & Well-being. *Learning from Practice: A Professional Development Text for Legal Externs*, 3rd ed., ed. Leah Wortham, Alexander Scherr, Nancy Maurer, and Susan L. Brooks. St. Paul: West Academic Publishing.

3

COMPETENCE AS A PROFESSIONAL VIRTUE

INTRODUCTION

We now turn from the introductory chapters to six chapters that each discusses one of the six virtues of the professional lawyer. For each virtue, we will describe what it means for lawyers, discuss challenges you may encounter in cultivating and deploying it, and offer suggestions for ways that you can acquire and then continue to develop it. We begin with the virtue of competence.

WHAT DOES "COMPETENCE" MEAN FOR LAWYERS?

Competence sounds simple enough. It seems to set up a minimal standard, but in fact it goes far beyond the minimum. Most professionalism codes and creeds describe what we are calling the virtue of competence as a matter of "excellence" or "craftsmanship." Competence as a virtue, therefore, requires much more than merely acceptable performance. The virtue of competence includes the specialized knowledge and skills of the legal professional, but it is not limited to those. It involves personal attributes such as relationship skills, resilience, integrity, and honesty, as well as recognition that continued development of competence is a lifelong task. Competence requires good legal judgment, as well as an understanding and appreciation of the complex world in which we live. We will start with what the Model Rules of Professional Conduct have to say about competence.

The requirements of Model Rules 1.1 and 1.3

Model Rules 1.1 and 1.3 capture some of the crucial components of the virtue of competence. Rule 1.1 requires lawyers to render competent representation and states that "[c]ompetent representation requires the legal knowledge, skill, thoroughness and preparation reasonably necessary for the representation." Rule 1.3 doubles down on thoroughness and preparation by requiring lawyers to "act with reasonable diligence and promptness in representing a client." The baseline for competence, therefore, includes three components: knowledge, skill, and diligence. The conciseness of those three requirements masks the complexity of lawyer competence, however. For within knowledge, skills, and diligence lie a broad range of attributes that truly define the competent lawyer.

Knowledge

As a law student, you have a special appreciation for the role of legal knowledge. You spend most of your time in law school learning basic principles of law. In your first-year courses, you learn foundational principles of contract, tort, property, and criminal and procedural law. In your upper-level courses, you expand into more specialized subjects. The knowledge required by Rule 1.1 is the knowledge "reasonably necessary for the representation," and thus the depth of knowledge required is a function of the complexity of the subject matter.

As a lawyer, the process of learning will continue. The comments to Rule 1.1 contemplate that you can undertake a matter that you are not initially competent to handle as long as you undertake the "necessary study." The jurisdiction in which you practice is highly likely to make your continued licensure as a lawyer contingent upon compliance with continuing legal education requirements. The acquisition of the knowledge you need to be competent starts in law school, but it never ends.

Skill

The second requirement of Rule 1.1 is the skill necessary for the representation. That could mean almost anything. But the comments to Rule 1.1 provide some guidance to the kinds of skills the rule requires. Comment 2 mentions analysis of precedent, legal drafting, and issue spotting. These examples indicate that Rule 1.1's skill requirement is about the expert techniques that you acquire by your specialized legal training.

Several leading studies have detailed the expert techniques needed to be an effective lawyer. In 1992, the American Bar Association (ABA) Section of Legal Education and Admission to the Bar issued the MacCrate Report, which identified the following necessary lawyer skills: problem solving, legal analysis and reasoning, legal research, factual investigation, communication, counseling, negotiation, organization and management of legal work (including control of workload and use of staff), and recognizing and resolving ethical dilemmas (Section of Legal Education and Admission to the Bar 1992). More recently, Professors Shultz and Zedeck identified 26 skills possessed by the most effective lawyers, including research and information gathering, communications, planning and organization, conflict resolution, and client/business relations (Shultz and Zedeck 2009).

As we explain later in this chapter, the set of skills required in order to claim the virtue of competence is broader than these lists of expert lawyerly techniques, but they serve as a good start for helping you understand what you will need to be able to do as a lawyer.

Diligence

Diligence requires close attention to detail and consistent application of your best efforts to the situation at hand, and as a law student you are familiar with how important it is. Comment 1 to Rule 1.3 recites that as a lawyer you must act with "commitment and dedication to the interests of the client and with zeal in advocacy upon the client's behalf" and that you must pursue the client's matter "despite opposition, obstruction, or personal inconvenience." Comment 2 specifically requires that you must control your workload, and comment 3 warns against procrastination. In fact, the importance of diligence is often best appreciated when it is absent, such as when a lawyer misses a deadline, provides legal advice without having read the relevant documents, or abandons a client. The absence of diligence often results in harm to a client. If you ever wondered why your professors insist upon daily diligent preparation and the meeting of all deadlines, now perhaps you can see how important that training is for your future career.

Note that a habit of procrastination can prevent diligence. Many busy people work against deadlines, and lawyers are not immune to that temptation. However, the duty of competence informs lawyers that procrastination is not acceptable. Postponing attention to a client matter until just before the deadline will prevent the thoroughness required. Many legal matters do not have externally imposed deadlines, which makes it easier to procrastinate. Even without a deadline, however, the competent lawyer will have the discipline and habit to complete work in a timely manner, including allowing sufficient time for unplanned contingencies.

Beyond the Model Rules of Professional Conduct

The rules of conduct are a good place to start to understand the virtue of competence, but the process cannot end there. There is much more to achieving "excellence" or to practicing with "craftsmanship" than knowing the law, learning technique and working hard. The virtue of competence also requires that you develop certain skills that go beyond technique. Professor Neil Hamilton's survey of major law firms and the professionalism literature reveals that, in addition to legal knowledge, lawyers are expected to possess both relational capacities and good character. The relational skills include such things as the ability to work with clients and with others, including teamwork, listening skills, and a service orientation to clients. The survey shows that lawyers are also expected to demonstrate personal skills such as resilience, integrity and honesty, initiative, and a commitment to continued self-improvement (Hamilton 2013). Three particular skills that you will also need are good judgment, emotional intelligence, and cultural competence and inclusive thinking.

Judgment

We will have much more to say about judgment in Chapter 8 on practical wisdom. For now, understand that the most valuable thing you will have to offer clients is your judgment, the expert answer to the hardest question a client can ask: "what should I do?" As a professional, you will almost always be operating in an environment of inherent uncertainty and competing goals. While some legal problems fall into categories of clear right and wrong, most do not. Rather, there are better and worse solutions, and there are better and worse ways of acting to achieve the solution. In other words, the successful lawyer must possess the skill of good professional judgment, including not only knowing the right thing to do, but being able to do the right thing in the right way. Ethical and effective professional action is dependent upon good legal judgment.

Emotional intelligence

Although it may be hard to tell this from your law school experience so far, being a lawyer is about more than black letter law. Most lawyers interact daily with other people, often in times of great stress and anxiety. Lawyers must learn to recognize and manage their own emotions, to discern the emotions and motivations of others, and to use information about emotions to guide decisions and advice. These abilities comprise your "emotional intelligence" and are part of your competence as a lawyer.

Think about a few examples when emotional intelligence will help you be a better lawyer. You may feel frustration when a judge rules against you or an opposing counsel obstructs a deposition with needless objections. Your emotions can get the better of you if you do not recognize that frustration in yourself and learn to manage it. Slamming your notes down on counsel table will not help you with the judge. Screaming at opposing counsel is never effective. This is why the study of "foundations for practice" by Educating Tomorrow's Lawyers found that three of the most important skills a lawyer needs from day one are "emotional regulation/self-control," "tact and diplomacy," and treating others with "courtesy and respect" (Educating Tomorrow's Lawyers 2016, 9).

Emotional intelligence will also help you discern others' emotions and motivations. You need to develop empathy, which refers broadly to the capacity or ability to imagine oneself in the situation of another, experiencing the emotions, ideas, or opinions of that person. You must learn to be open to others and do your best to understand the situation from another's point of view. As the great fictional lawyer Atticus Finch put it, "You don't really know someone until you get inside his skin and walk around in it for a while" (Lee 1960, 30).

How does this make you a better lawyer? You will be a better counselor if you grasp what really matters to your client. You will be a better negotiator if you know what will motivate an opposing party or lawyer to make a deal. You will be a better advocate if you can frame your client's case in a way that lines up with how the jurors likely perceive the facts. The best lawyers can read people and understand them. It takes emotional intelligence to do that.

Cultural competence and inclusive thinking

The future of law practice is one of increasing diversity of clients and problems, as well as greater diversity of other lawyers, juries, and judges. As the world is becoming more diverse, our understanding of diversity is expanding. We are becoming much more aware of the ways in which people think, learn, and work differently. A competent lawyer must develop cultural competence and engage in inclusive thinking. A lawyer with cultural competence will possess an in-depth understanding of how to effectively and respectfully interact with people from a wide range of cultures, which requires being aware of one's own world view, developing positive attitudes towards cultural differences, and gaining knowledge of different cultural practices and world views. Moreover, the skill of inclusive thinking is the commitment and ability to include multiple perspectives in solving problems.

WHAT GETS IN THE WAY OF LAWYER COMPETENCE?

Excessive caseloads

Students often do not realize how many clients a busy lawyer has at any given time. The problem with juggling many responsibilities is that you might neglect to do something, and, if you do, harm to the client may ensue. Too many lawyers try to handle too many matters at the same time. You simply will be unable to devote the time and attention necessary to serve every client if you take on, or are assigned, too many responsibilities.

How does a caseload get excessive? In private practice it often arises early in a lawyer's career from fear—the fear that, if you decline to take on a client, you may never get another one. Before you know it, you may find that you have more to do than any one person could do diligently or well. A caseload can also grow beyond a manageable size because the lawyer is assigned too much work by another. An associate working for a firm may feel powerless to say no, for fear of losing a job. An assistant public defender may be appointed to represent too many defendants because there are numerous defendants and only a few public defenders. In fact, in some jurisdictions public defenders have refused to represent new clients because they were trying to protect their ability to serve existing clients.

Even the smartest and hardest-working lawyer only has 24 hours in a day. Too many clients can lead to not enough competence.

Fear of inadequacy or unpleasant tasks

In addition to the economic fear that can lead to excessive caseloads, other types of fear can lead to incompetence through avoidance and therefore neglect of the client's case. Fear may stem from a feeling of inadequacy or from not knowing how to handle a difficult client, with the result that the lawyer feels overwhelmed by the matter. Sometimes, the lawyer reacts by avoiding the situation, which results in putting off tasks that are difficult or unpleasant. The lawyer may avoid working at all on a particularly difficult case, avoid communicating with a difficult client, or let fear impede contacting a client with bad news.

The relationship between fear and the absence of competence explains why this can be a particular problem for inexperienced attorneys. As a newer attorney, you may not recognize that you are not sufficiently knowledgeable or skilled to take on a client matter, resulting in overconfidence. Or you may fail to appreciate the complexity of a particular matter because of lack of experience. You may realize that you lack the knowledge or skills for a matter, but don't know what to do about it, or where to turn. As a new attorney, you lack the experience of having dealt with similar situations in the past.

It is normal to experience some fear. In fact, it would be unusual if you did not, given the complexities and uncertainties of being a lawyer. The lesson is that you must handle fear appropriately by acknowledging it and seeking assistance rather than letting it lead to neglect of your professional responsibilities. This may be a particular challenge if you are in solo practice, because you may lack the ready availability of colleagues or mentors that comes from practicing within a more collective setting. One way to handle your fear is to seek out and learn from mentors. As we explain below, this may take some effort on your part, but it is worth it.

Lack of mentoring

The law has a long and grand tradition of mentoring. Law school can only do so much, even with knowledge and technique, and young lawyers have traditionally learned how to practice law in the practical, day-to-day world by watching and emulating experienced lawyers. Especially for advanced competencies like good judgment, mentors are essential.

There is widespread sentiment that the mentoring tradition in the law has been eroding for some time. That perception has driven some states to mandate a period of formal mentoring upon admission to the bar. These efforts are laudable but are a symptom that the tradition may survive only if lawyers are forced to be mentored. There is no easy explanation for why the tradition of mentoring in the law is threatened. One theory is that, when the size of the bar expanded exponentially in the 1960s and 1970s, there simply were not enough mentors to go around. Economic pressures—the perceived need to bill every hour of the work day—may also lead lawyers not to spend time on an unbillable activity like mentoring. The increased tendency of lawyers to move from firm to firm reduces the possibility of any economic return on the careful and costly mentoring of young lawyers. Whatever the cause, a lack of mentoring feeds on itself. Those who are not mentored do not understand the need for it or how to do it. Those who are not mentored often do not mentor. This avenue for nurturing the developing competence of young lawyers does not happen as easily as it previously did.

Over-emphasis in law school on legal knowledge and technique

In law school, as you may have noticed, the emphasis is on learning the law and, to a somewhat lesser extent, learning some basic techniques of lawyering. But as we have seen, being a competent lawyer requires much more, although you would not discern that from the typical law school curriculum. In fact, as we mentioned in Chapter 2, studies show that law students tend to drift away from their original motivations for coming to law school, which many applicants would describe as a desire to make a difference in the world and in the lives of others. Law students also report that law school causes them to feel disassociated from relationships that mattered when law school began. They are taught to disregard how they feel to focus on the facts and law. Cognition crowds out feeling. Emotional intelligence is not likely to flourish in such an environment. And cultural competence and inclusive thinking are only just now making their way into the curriculum.

Personal problems, mental illness, and substance use

The most common case of lack of competence by a lawyer involves an attorney who abandons multiple clients. The lawyer becomes unreachable and does not attend to what the clients need done. Statutes of limitations expire, cases get dismissed for failure to prosecute, or requests for admission go unanswered. These are extreme cases of lack of competence as lack of diligence.

A frequent and significant cause of incompetence and client neglect is things going wrong in a lawyer's personal life. A lawyer who is undergoing stressful personal events, such as divorce, a new family member, or death and illness of loved ones, may not be able to devote the required attention to professional matters. Sometimes those personal stresses manifest themselves in physical or mental illness, particularly depression, and substance use. As you saw in Chapter 2, lawyers experience a high rate of depression and substance use, which in turn results in a downward spiral of client neglect and lack of competence.

Whether they involve personal problems, mental illness, or substance use, these can be stories of personal tragedy—here we simply note that the tragedies can cause collateral damage to the clients of these lawyers by impairing the lawyer's competence.

Inadequacy of external enforcement of the duty of competence

You might initially take some comfort in the fact that there are numerous external processes that seek to promote competence and deter its opposite. The bar exam supposedly ensures that only competent candidates become lawyers, and, as you have seen, competence is required by the rules of conduct. Lawyers are also subject to malpractice actions if they provide incompetent representation. In the specific context of criminal defense, the doctrine of ineffective assistance of counsel exists to protect defendants from incompetence. That initial sense of comfort is misplaced—each of these external controls has severe limitations.

The bar exam falls short of providing a complete external assurance of competence. It is likely that you will be required to take the Multistate Bar Exam (MBE), which consists of 200 multiple choice questions that cover civil procedure, constitutional law, contracts, criminal law and procedure, evidence, real property, and torts. The MBE tests basic knowledge of these subjects but no others. A multiple-choice exam cannot hope to test any of the necessary legal techniques such as research, writing, and counseling, nor can it test any of the other skills we have identified as necessary for your competence.

You also likely will take the Multistate Practice Test (MPT). The MPT includes two 90-minute questions that will call upon you to work with a given set of facts and a "library" of cases, regulations and statutes. You will be assigned to produce a particular type of document, such as a memo to a supervising lawyer, a letter to a client, or a closing argument. The MPT tests for aspects of competence that the MBE does not, including especially legal analysis and writing. It does not, however, reach other necessary skills such as research, interviewing, emotional intelligence, cultural competence, or inclusive thinking.

Finally, your bar exam will probably include most of a day of writing essay answers to questions particularly about the state law in your jurisdiction. This part of the exam will test specific aspects of legal knowledge (whatever your bar examiners pick for that exam), as well as your writing skills. It will not test any other aspect of your competence.

The disciplinary process and the prospect of malpractice liability also will not act as external assurances of competence. Although competence is a duty imposed by the rules of professional conduct, lawyers are almost never disciplined for incompetent performance, with the exception of a lack of diligence. Proving a lawyer did not have the requisite knowledge or skill for a particular matter is much more difficult than proving the lawyer missed deadlines or abandoned a matter. Perhaps because of this difficulty, bar counsel tend to count on the availability of malpractice actions by clients to be the external check on attorney competence. But malpractice is an incomplete remedy at best. A client must first realize that the lawyer has engaged in incompetent practice. That will not be detectable or apparent to many clients. The client also must have suffered sufficient damage that another lawyer will be willing to take on the malpractice action. Much incompetence that does not cause significant harm goes unaddressed. And a malpractice action usually makes economic sense only if the lawyer has malpractice insurance, and currently only two states require it. Neither the fear of discipline nor the fear of a malpractice judgment provides an external check on a lack of knowledge or skill.

The doctrine of ineffective assistance of counsel is another external check on competence. Although it does not result in any direct sanction on an ineffective lawyer, it presumably carries a reputational cost—no one wants to be declared "ineffective" by a court. But in practice the doctrine is glaringly incomplete as a way of ensuring competence in criminal defense. In *Strickland v. Washington*, 466 U.S. 668 (1984), the Supreme Court of the United States held that anyone claiming ineffective assistance must satisfy two "prongs." The first is that the lawyer's representation must have been unreasonable, but *Strickland* instructs courts to approach this question with enormous deference to a lawyer's "tactical" choices. Almost anything can be labeled as "tactical." Even when a court detects unreasonable performance, there is no remedy unless the court also finds that there is a substantial probability that the result of the case would have been different if the defense lawyer had been competent. Many a defendant has received no redress because, although the defense lawyer was incompetent, there was enough evidence of guilt that the court was willing to say, in effect, "no harm, no foul."

Each of these measures relates to attorney competence. They are important and serve useful purposes. You must recognize, however, that you can obtain your license and keep it even if in many ways you are not competent, and that you mostly need not fear a malpractice suit or a finding of ineffective assistance of counsel. Your motivation to become and remain competent will have to come from a source other than fear of punishment.

Implicit bias

As we have seen, cultural competence and inclusive thinking are necessary to your competence. A particular barrier that you may need to overcome is implicit bias. Scientific studies reveal that everyone possesses implicit biases—ways of thinking that cause the brain to rely on shortcuts rather than a lengthier reasoning process. That may be helpful in some situations, such as when you recognize quickly what a stop sign means when you are driving. However, other shortcuts are not benign—those that rely on such characteristics as race, sex, customs of dress, and the like. Everyone relies on implicit biases, and some of them will get in the way of your being a good lawyer. To overcome that challenge, you must be aware of the limitations of your own perspective and of your implicit biases and make a commitment to developing skills that will move you beyond them.

STRATEGIES FOR CULTIVATING THE VIRTUE OF COMPETENCE

Cultivate a habit of honoring commitments

A first step for a lawyer who wants competence to be part of his or her professional identity is to develop the habit of honoring commitments. You would not want a lawyer who did not show up for a meeting with you, or a court appearance for you, or one who was late to either a meeting or a court appearance. You would not want a lawyer who would forget or disregard a filing deadline for a court or who otherwise would neglect to accomplish tasks for you in a diligent and timely manner.

Timeliness and diligence are virtues that will take you closer to the goal of being a professional lawyer. Honoring commitments is what you *do* as a professional lawyer, but it should be easy to see how that habit eventually morphs into who you *are*. The initial resolution, "I will honor my commitments," translates into action. Commitments are made and met. Deadlines are calendared and observed. Files are organized and work is managed. Such repeated, habitual action gradually becomes a matter of your identity. Eventually, you will say, "I am the kind of lawyer who honors my commitments." The virtues of timeliness and diligence become internalized at a deep level. You no longer have to think each time a task is undertaken, "I need to be careful to accomplish this is a timely and diligent manner." Doing so has become second nature. You will deploy the virtues of timeliness and diligence without conscious thought.

How do you, as a law student, cultivate the habit of "honoring commitments"? You show up in class. You arrive on time. You come to class prepared. You do your work diligently throughout the semester, so that there is no need of cramming at the end. You do not allow distractions, social or otherwise, to come between you and the fulfillment of your commitments as a student. Law school requires that you study harder and better than you have ever studied before, and in the process it forces you to develop habits of diligence and timeliness that lead to the fulfillment of your commitments. Those habits eventually become part of who you are. You become the kind of law student who is in class, every day, on time, ready to participate and learn. Those habits, and that identity, will transfer to your life as a lawyer.

Responsibly manage workload and financial obligations

Lawyers must be habitually realistic about how much time and effort matters will take and how much time and energy are available. Begin to develop the habit of time and workload management in law school. You will have many opportunities for involvement in extracurricular activities, networking events, public service, paid or unpaid work, and social involvement, all on top of your academic requirements. It can be tempting to say "yes" to every opportunity because so many of them are worthwhile. But as you may have discovered, over-commitment can impair your ability to be prepared for class and to meet other academic responsibilities.

That overabundance of opportunities awaits you after graduation as well. It is not just that you may have too many potential clients. The community and the profession are likely to demand your time and attention. In fact, one of the pleasures of being a lawyer is that your knowledge and skills will make you highly sought after for such service. We encourage your involvement in those kinds of meaningful activities, but you need to begin now to recognize that you cannot do everything. You need to develop the self-awareness to prioritize where and how you want to spend your limited time and energy. Taking on too much, even with the best intent, will result in not being able to do it all, or perhaps anything, well. Practice saying "no" in a way that does not leave bad feelings and that may leave the door open for future opportunities with the organization or potential client you are turning down.

You can start now. Practice how you will say no to an extra-curricular activity, for example,

> *Right now, I've chosen to devote a lot of time and energy to moot court; I admire what your organization stands for and would love to contribute in the future, but I could not devote sufficient time and attention because of my other commitments.*

Realize that saying "no" is not selfish, although it may at first feel that way; it is in fact a critical part of your professional identity that will make you a good lawyer. Developing the habit in law school of carefully managing your time will help you in the future to manage your time as a lawyer and ensure that you do not spread yourself so thin that your competence suffers.

Your ability to manage your workload as a lawyer is also dependent upon your ability to manage your financial obligations. Most of us work at least in part because we need the income that work brings. For lawyers in private practice, that income comes from clients. As we have noted, many lawyers take on too much because of their concern that they cannot afford to turn down any available work. For lawyers in public service or who work in the corporate sector, the source of income is an employer, and you may have to make the hard decision to leave a job if it is not allowing you to practice law with competence. Begin to develop the habit of financial responsibility in law school so that it is a habit that you take into your life as a lawyer. Educate yourself about financial management; take advantage of courses such as law office management that will help you understand the business realities of law practice. Set realistic financial goals and earn the autonomy that will enable you to turn down additional work if it would erode your competence. We acknowledge how difficult this can be for the vast majority of you who have significant student loans to repay, but those loans are all the more reason to plan your financial future carefully and realistically.

Commit to well-being and self-care

Commitment to well-being and self-care is essential to your fulfilling the duty of competence. It is, therefore, a professional responsibility. If personal problems, depression, or substance use are impairing your ability to represent clients competently, then it is your responsibility to address those issues.

But well-being is about much more than that: it is about your capacity to truly experience the satisfaction that can come from a highly fulfilling, albeit highly demanding, profession. As we saw in Chapter 2, the ABA National Task Force on Lawyer Well-Being defined well-being as thriving in multiple dimensions of your life, including social, emotional, spiritual, intellectual, physical, and occupational. Well-being is about more than the absence of illness, and it is not synonymous with feeling happy all the time. Rather, it is an ability to cope with the stresses of life, to reach one's potential, to work productively, and to contribute to one's community. Well-being will support your competence as a lawyer and do much more.

Studies have shown that there are several reasons for lawyers' failure to maintain well-being and to be particularly susceptible to depression and substance use. This research helps us understand what you can do in law school to begin to develop the habits that will help you reach these goals as a lawyer.

First, self-awareness is key. Understand that law school is a competitive environment and that it creates stresses for you to which you may be unaccustomed. As we have seen, law school can shift your focus from the long-term goals that made you want to be a lawyer and place undue emphasis on short-term goals such as grades, journal membership, academic honors or awards, and the first job after graduation. It can place time demands on you that cause you to neglect important relationships, activities that bring you enjoyment, healthy eating and sleeping habits, and physical exercise. It can also attack your self-confidence and create an environment in which you are fearful of showing self-doubt or lack of knowledge.

So, first, practice self-awareness and the habit of reflection. Expect and acknowledge that at the same time that you are experiencing the positive side of law school—such as an increase in knowledge and skills, meeting new people, focusing on your future as a lawyer—there will be some negative pressures with which you must deal. Use that self-awareness to remind yourself of your long-term goals and to focus on how law school can help you achieve them. Set aside time to reflect upon the ways in which your developing knowledge and skills are affecting those goals and adjust to new areas of interest or to new self-knowledge that will help you choose the right career path.

Second, develop and practice relationship skills. This includes setting aside time to take care of relationships with important people in your life whom you knew before law school. Manage your workload so that you can have time with your family and friends. You should also use the opportunity of law school to create new relationships with classmates, faculty and staff at the law school, and lawyers with whom you come into contact through law school activities. Many studies show that meaningful relationships are an important antidote to stress, and that it is difficult to experience well-being in the absence of fulfilling relationships with other people. And as you saw in Chapter 2, Self-Determination Theory teaches us that *relatedness* is one of your basic psychological needs.

Third, develop habits of activities that sustain physical and mental health. That includes taking the time to eat healthy meals, get enough rest, and engage in physical exercise and leisure activities. These are important to your continuing to live an authentic and healthy life. Such activities contribute to both physical and mental/emotional well-being. Yet they can seem like optional time commitments among the many required commitments of law school. Begin the habit of integrating time for both types of activities in your daily and weekly calendars so that they become habits.

Finally, use your commitment to well-being to seek help when you feel you need it. It can be very difficult to admit the need for help in a highly charged competitive environment such as law school or the legal profession. The good news is that there has never been greater understanding of the reasons for law student and lawyer distress and of how to overcome it. Every law school offers resources for helping students, including access to low-cost or free mental health treatment. You can access those resources through the dean of students or any faculty member. Many law school student bar associations have developed well-being programs that provide resources and support for law students attempting to counter the stresses of law school. There are good online resources as well through the ABA or state bar websites and other sites devoted to well-being.

Do not fear that seeking help will negatively affect your ability to become a lawyer. In fact, neglecting your physical and mental well-being is more likely to be an impediment to bar admission. State bar admissions processes, including those for character and fitness certification, are supportive of students getting the help they need and will be affirming of those efforts.

Develop skills of emotional intelligence, cultural competence, and inclusive thinking

Your development of emotional intelligence, cultural competence, and inclusive thinking will happen over time. It can be very difficult to truly see the world through another's eyes or to understand a culture very different from your own. Research shows that the ability to do so is gained over an extended period and with ongoing practice and reflection.

You can begin now to develop awareness and habits that will support your becoming more empathetic and culturally competent. Seek out perspectives that are different from your own so that you are able to see the world through others' eyes and to take multiple perspectives into account as you approach clients and solve legal problems. This is a difficult thing for humans to do. We are all products of our own experiences, which in turn shape the way that we interact with others and view the world. A lawyer cannot be competent, however, without the self-awareness that his or her perspective is not universally shared and without the commitment to overcome the kind of narrow thinking that comes from relying only on one's perspective.

Expand your personal and professional networks to include greater diversity. In law school, take advantage of opportunities to be with students whose views and experiences are different than yours. Learn about student organizations that represent different viewpoints and experiences than yours. Do not live in a bubble—get out of your comfort zone. Likewise, once you become a lawyer, seek out workplace environments where those with whom you will be working are diverse and where you will work for diverse clients. Find a work environment that shares your commitment to cultural competence and inclusive thinking. Take advantage of the many resources for lawyers and other professionals about emotional intelligence, cultural competence, and inclusive thinking. As a law student those include courses and extracurricular opportunities; as a lawyer, use CLE opportunities to continue your development.

Develop resilience and grit

Just as lawyers are benefitting from research on the connection between well-being and competence, there is now evidence that qualities of resilience and grit will support being a competent lawyer. Resilience refers to durability in the face of adversity, including the ability to bounce back when you have experienced something negative or traumatic. Resilience is the ability to overcome adversity with minimal long-term effects. Studies show that resilience is more likely when one has social connections and an attitude of realistic optimism. Conversely, resilience is undermined when one has a skeptical or pessimistic mindset and when one is socially isolated.

Grit is a related concept, defined as passion and perseverance in the pursuit of important long-term goals. A lawyer with grit will have developed the ability to see the long-term while adapting to the short-term. Gritty and resilient people exhibit optimism and a strong sense that they are able to positively impact their own circumstances. They are able to be flexible in the face of negative events and often see opportunity to grow from adversity. They are able to accept constructive criticism and to learn from it. Milana Hogan's study of grit and lawyers revealed a connection between professional success and lawyers who exhibited growth mindset and grit (Hogan 2017).

These qualities are important in all contexts, but they are particularly critical in a demanding and adversarial profession such as law, in which lawyers are often working with people in difficult situations. You are going to fail sometimes as a lawyer. That does not mean that you are incompetent. It is the nature of the life you have chosen. Accept that fact and resolve not to let it get you down. The good news is that resilience and grit are not inherent characteristics that some people have and others lack. While they may come more easily to some people, they can be developed by all.

The literature on ways in which lawyers can develop resilience and grit is still evolving; however, there are some results that show that the following are helpful steps.

First, resilience and grit are contagious. You will be more likely to display them when you are around others who have them. Therefore, seek out people who seem to be able to overcome adversity and to keep their long-term goals in sight even in the middle of short-term demands. Similarly, resilience and grit flow from positive relationships with family, friends, and peers. The positive relationships include mutual, reciprocal support and caring. These types of relationships help strengthen a person's resilience, just as they support well-being.

Second, exercise mindfulness to learn to view negative experiences as opportunities for growth and change. This does not mean that you will never perceive events as negative. Indeed, realistic optimism is what is called for—the most resilient people understand the reality of a negative situation. The optimism that marks resilience does not mean that in every situation you simply deny that negative things are happening. Rather, resilient people look for a silver lining. By cultivating a habit of approaching situations in this way, you can avoid what is called "learned helplessness" and will increase your ability to move from negative to positive outcomes—perhaps all the way to "learned optimism" (Seligman 2006).

Third, look for ways to find purpose and meaning in what you are doing. Staying in touch with the purposes for which you came to law school, or, after graduation, with the larger purposes of your legal career, will help you to focus on the long term, even while doing what is necessary to meet short-term requirements and goals.

Cultivate habits of reflection and self-awareness

Closely related to grit are the habits of reflection and self-awareness, which are necessary to learning from experience. You live in the fastest-paced culture the world has ever known. Stopping long enough to breathe, much less to reflect, may not be part of your routine. But as a student and as a lawyer, your performance will improve if you take the time to pay attention and reflect on your work and its consequences. Begin now to develop habits of reflection and self-awareness that will allow you to continually grow in your acquisition of knowledge, skills, and values.

Educational psychology shows that those who learn from past experience do so because of their capacity to reflect upon past experience, then to adjust new experiences to what they've learned through reflection, and then to engage in new experiences in an improved manner based upon what they have learned. Without the capacity for reflection, you will be stuck in a repetitive cycle of behavior. The lawyer who does not have a habit of reflection is unlikely to improve and will not benefit from successes or failures.

Reflection can be difficult because it makes us come face to face with our mistakes or uncertainties. But it is also affirming when we realize what we did well in a particular situation and think about the ways that we can adapt what we did well to a new, changed situation.

Developing the capacity for reflection includes being open to receiving feedback and to using that feedback for continual improvement. Initially, the prospect of feedback can be frightening, and its receipt can be disheartening. A draft memo or brief that comes back with red ink all over it may bring you down a notch. But feedback is essential. Embrace it—you are a novice, and you have much to learn. Feedback from your professors and mentors is how you get better.

As a law student, you have multiple opportunities for feedback on your developing lawyering skills. Those opportunities don't end upon graduation, however. Seek and use opportunities as a lawyer to receive feedback and, then, to use it to improve.

Use your experience to continue to develop your legal judgment

Humans develop good judgment over time, with the accumulation of experiences and exposure to role models who exercise good judgment. Lawyers acquire good legal judgment in the same way—by accumulating legal experiences and learning both from their own experiences and, importantly, from experiences of other lawyers. Those who have studied the ways in which people develop good judgment consistently note the importance of exemplars from whom to learn. In other words, one of the best ways to develop good legal judgment is to learn from those who have it. That opportunity doesn't come along by accident. You can make it happen by being intentional about two things: first, seek out good lawyers and, second, make a conscious effort to learn from them. Begin in law school to make connections with lawyers. When you make choices about where to work, whether during school or afterwards, consider whether the other lawyers with whom you will be working are ones from whom you can learn. Seek out mentors, within your own law practice setting or elsewhere. The old saying is that good judgment cannot be taught, but it can be learned. You can kick-start the process.

Watch what good lawyers do that demonstrates good judgment. Learn, too, from their mistakes. If you see something that didn't go well, think about the cause and what could have been done differently. Ask lawyers about their lives and what they've learned. You may be surprised to learn that most lawyers are pleased to help newer members of the profession by sharing their experiences and reflecting upon them.

Remember to focus on the rewards of developing and maintaining competence

As you have seen, external controls on your competence are incomplete at best. The bar exam, bar discipline, and the doctrines of malpractice and ineffective assistance of counsel all together do not provide much external assurance of your competence. Why, then, should you undertake the necessary efforts to become and remain competent?

Recall from Chapter 2 that there are different kinds of motivations for your conduct. A fear of discipline is an extrinsic motivation. As you have seen, that by itself will not be enough with respect to competence (or, as you will see, with respect to any of the other virtues). The other types of motivations, however, *intrinsic motivations* and *identified motivations*, stand a much better chance of doing the job.

Take *intrinsic motivation* first. Think about some difficult skill you have mastered in the past. It was difficult, but once you mastered it and engaged in it at a high level, it was rewarding *for its own sake*. That will be true for you once you master aspects of the practice of law. One of the rewards for being excellent in your profession will be that deep sense of mastery. Remember also that Self-Determination Theory teaches us that competence is one of the three basic psychological needs. Virtue ethics leads you to the same place. The only way for you to obtain the "internal goods" of the practice of law is to practice in accordance with the standards of the practice, and competence is one of them.

Now consider *identified motivation*, which causes you to act in service to something deeply valued even if the activity is not rewarding for its own sake. It serves another fundamental purpose. As you mature as a lawyer, your service to your clients even at personal cost should become something you deeply value. It should become an *identified motivation* that will lead you to cultivate competence—your ability to serve—even when the activity is not rewarding for its own sake.

CONCLUSION

Your professional identity of a lawyer must include an internalized personal commitment to the acquisition, cultivation and deployment of competence in all of its forms. For that to happen, you must understand what competence means and the reasons why lawyers sometimes do not act competently. You then need to cultivate good habits that will support your resolve to serve with the competence that your clients deserve.

DISCUSSION QUESTIONS AND PROBLEMS

1   Suppose you are five years out of law school and have been in general practice in your hometown since graduation. Your practice experience has been fairly evenly divided among estate planning, domestic relations, defense of civil cases on behalf of several insurance company clients, and general business matters. You have on three occasions reviewed franchise agreements on behalf of clients who were seeking your advice about whether they should become franchisees of national companies. You have never represented a franchisor. You are now approached by a couple whom you have met through community activities. The couple has been running a very successful local coffee shop for three years, and they would like to hire you to help them franchise the coffee shop nationally. Are you competent to take on the representation? What factors affect your decision? If you are not now competent to agree to the representation, what steps could you take to avoid turning down the business?

2   Think of a time in your life when you didn't perform as well as you could have on a task or assignment. What were the reasons that you didn't? For example, was the problem a failure to plan appropriately, procrastination, not being able to work well with someone else, or something else? What could you have done differently to have performed better? What steps can you take in the future to avoid this happening again?

3   Choose a week in your upcoming schedule. List the activities that you must or would like to engage in during that week, such as work and school demands, spending time with friends and/or family, physical exercise, leisure activities, extracurricular commitments, and anything else that needs to happen during that time. Make a schedule that sets out how you will accomplish all of those things. Is it realistic? Does the amount of time you are spending on each task represent its priority in your life? Use this exercise to assess whether you can better manage your time in the future, and if so, create a plan for doing so.

4   Arrange an informal interview with a lawyer you know or recommended by your law school's faculty or staff. Ask the lawyer about the early years of their practice and how they dealt with acquiring the experience they needed to increase their competence. Ask them whether they ever encountered a situation in which they were asked to take on a representation that they did not feel competent to handle and what they did. Ask them about ways in which they continue to develop their competence and stay current on developments in the law, technology, or law practice. Ask them for any advice about how you can continue to develop competence as a new lawyer and what to do when you feel that you lack the competence to handle a matter.

5   We have identified skills such as emotional intelligence, grit, cultural competency, and inclusive thinking as necessary for the competent lawyer. We have also acknowledged that these skills are not usually taught in the traditional law school classroom. Make a list of five concrete activities in which you can engage while in law school that would help you to acquire these skills and commit to doing one or more of them over the remainder of your legal education.

6   Several surveys of lawyers have identified teamwork as an essential skill for a competent lawyer. Yet most law school courses do not teach or assess teamwork. Reflect on whether you have learned teamwork skills during your legal education. If you have not, identify ways that you can do so before graduation. For example, can you take advantage of courses (clinical or simulated skills courses) or extracurricular activities in which teamwork is fostered, or use summer work experiences to gain experience working in teams?

7   We have discussed the importance of learning from experience, including the ways in which experts learn from reflection upon experience. Remember a time when you did not do something as well as you would have liked. For example, did you perform more poorly than you would have liked on a law school writing assignment or an in-class exercise, or did you have a disappointing interaction with a friend or family member? Take some time to reflect upon what you can learn from the experience: what went well and what could you have done better? For example, could you have listened more carefully to the assignment or to the person with whom you were talking? Could you have begun working on the assignment or exercise earlier, or not been so quick to react in your social interaction? Make a list of what you can do differently the next time you encounter a similar situation and commit to incorporating what you've learned into your future conduct. Then, the next time that you are in a similar situation, be intentional about incorporating those suggestions and reflecting afterwards about whether your performance was improved as a result.

REFERENCE LIST AND SUGGESTED READINGS

American Bar Association Diversity and Inclusion Center. 2019. *Toolkit on Implicit Bias*. www.american-bar.org/groups/diversity/resources/implicit-bias/.

American Bar Association National Task Force on Lawyer Well-Being. 2018. *The Path to Lawyer Well-Being: Practical Recommendations for Positive Change, the Report from the National Task Force on Lawyer Well-Being*. Chicago: American Bar Association.

American Bar Association Section of Legal Education and Admissions to the Bar. 1992. *Report of the Task Force on Law Schools and the Profession: Narrowing the Gap, Legal Education and Professional Development—An Educational Continuum* (commonly known as the MacCrate Report). www.americanbar.org/content/dam/aba/publications/misc/legal_education/2013_legal_education_and_professional_development_maccrate_report).authcheckdam.pdf.

Bryant, Susan. 2001. *The Five Habits: Building Cross-Cultural Competence in Lawyers*. http://academicworks.cuny.edu/cl_pubs/258.

Duckworth, Angela. 2016. *Grit: The Power of Passion and Perseverance*. New York: Scribner.

Educating Tomorrow's Lawyers. 2016. *The Whole Lawyer and the Character Quotient*. https://iaals.du.edu/sites/default/files/documents/publications/foundations_for_practice_whole_lawyer_character_quotient.pdf.

Floyd, Daisy Hurst. 2013. The Authentic Lawyer: Merging the Personal and the Professional. *Essential Qualities of the Professional Lawyer*, ed. Paul A. Haskins. Chicago: ABA Publishing.

Floyd, Daisy Hurst, and Timothy W. Floyd. 2016. Professional Identity and Formation. *Learning from Practice: A Text for Experiential Legal Education*, 3rd ed., ed. Leah Wortham, Alexander Scherr, Nancy Maurer, and Susan L. Brooks. St. Paul: West Academic Publishing.

Goleman, Daniel. 2012. *Emotional Intelligence: Why It Can Matter More Than IQ*. New York: Bantam Dell.

Hamilton, Neil W. 2013. The Qualities of the Professional Lawyer. *Essential Qualities of the Professional Lawyer*, ed. Paul A. Haskins. Chicago: ABA Publishing.

Henderson, William D. 2013. Successful Lawyer Skills and Behaviors. *Essential Qualities of the Professional Lawyer*, ed. Paul A. Haskins. Chicago: ABA Publishing.

Hogan, Milanda L. 2017. *Grit, The Secret to Advancement: Stories of Successful Women Lawyers*. Chicago: ABA Publishing.

Lee, Harper. 1960. *To Kill a Mockingbird*. United States of America: Warner Books.

Patel, Serena. 2014. Cultural Competency Theory: Preparing Law Students for Practice in Our Multicultural World. *UCLA L. Rev. Disc.* 62:140.

Reeves, Arin N. 2013. Inclusive Thinking. *Essential Qualities of the Professional Lawyer*, ed. Paul A. Haskins. Chicago: ABA Publishing.

Schon, Donald A. 1983. *The Reflective Practitioner: How Professionals Think in Action*. United States of America: Basic Books.

Seligman, Martin E.P. 2006. *Learned Optimism: How to Change Your Mind and Your Life*. New York: Vintage Press.

Shultz, Marjorie M., and Zedeck, Sheldon. 2009. *Predicting Lawyer Effectiveness: A New Assessment for Use in Law School Admission Decisions*. https://ssrn.com/abstract=1442118 or http://dx.doi.org/10.2139/ssrn.1442118.

Sisk, Gregory C. 2018. Duties to Effectively Represent the Client. *Legal Ethics and the Practice of Law*, ed. Gregory C. Sisk, Susan Saab Fortney, Charles Gardner Geyh, Neil W. Hamilton, William D. Henderson, Vincent R. Johnson, Katherine R. Kruse, Stephen L. Pepper, and Melissa H. Weresh. St. Paul: West Academic Publishing.

4

FIDELITY TO THE CLIENT
AS A PROFESSIONAL VIRTUE

INTRODUCTION

In Chapters 1 and 2, we emphasized that lawyers play an essential role in serving societal goals, including achieving justice. You will serve those goals primarily through the representation of your clients. Serving the client's interest, as the client perceives that interest, is the essence of representation. As a lawyer, you will offer independent judgment, but you will exercise that judgment primarily in order to serve the client. Perhaps you don't need that reminder; of course lawyers represent clients. But it is worth emphasizing that usually you will not be a free agent, working entirely independently to achieve societal goals. Fidelity to the client is an essential virtue if lawyers are to perform their valuable social role.

In legal terms, lawyers owe duties to their clients under the rules of conduct and under the law of fiduciary duty. These duties overlap to a great extent, and we group them as your general duty of "fidelity to the client." According to the New Shorter Oxford English Dictionary (1993), fidelity means "[l]oyalty, faithfulness, [and] unswerving allegiance." Fidelity to the client will often require subordinating your personal interests in favor of the client's. One of the hardest things for human being to do—including a law student or new lawyer—is to grow into a mindset that is other-oriented rather than self-oriented.

In addition to being faithful agents of their clients, lawyers are also, in the language of the Preamble to the Model Rules, "officers of the court and public citizens with a special responsibility for the quality of justice." For that reason, fidelity to the client is not an absolute value. Sometimes other duties will require you to temper your fidelity to the client. Lawyers are sometimes criticized for being "hired guns," for taking illegal actions on behalf of their clients, for turning a blind eye on client misdeeds, or for using abusive tactics in litigation. Sometimes that criticism is valid; some lawyers have committed gross misconduct in the name of fidelity to the client. Although loyalty is the cornerstone of lawyers' relationships with their clients, the lawyer's duty of loyalty may sometimes conflict with other lawyer virtues such as fidelity to the law or civility. It takes practical wisdom to resolve conflicts among professional virtues, especially in conditions of irreducible uncertainty.

But most often, lawyers serve the public interest through unswerving loyalty to clients within the bounds of the law, protecting the rights of clients, safeguarding client confidences, and offering independent judgment and counsel to clients. This chapter sets forth what fidelity to the client means, what can get in the way, and what habits you should cultivate as part of a disposition toward fidelity to the client.

WHAT DOES "FIDELITY TO THE CLIENT" MEAN?

Lawyers as fiduciaries of clients

Courts consistently hold that the relationship of lawyer to client is a fiduciary one. As a Comment to Section 16 of the Restatement (Third) of the Law Governing Lawyers (American Law Institute 2000, 146) puts it:

> *A lawyer is a fiduciary, that is, a person to whom another person's affairs are entrusted in circumstances that often make it difficult or undesirable for that other person to supervise closely the performance of the fiduciary. Assurances of the lawyer's competence, diligence, and loyalty are therefore vital.*

Lawyers are entrusted with their client's problems, and the law accordingly places high standards on the lawyer. In this sense, the law treats lawyers the same way it deals with other fiduciaries such as executors and trustees, and for much the same reason. Executors, trustees, and lawyers are entrusted with other people's affairs (and often their money and property as well), under circumstances in which the beneficiary or client has no choice but to trust the good faith, integrity, and competence of the fiduciary. In the archaic (but still often quoted) language of Justice Cardozo, a fiduciary

> *is held to something stricter than the morals of the market place. Not honesty alone, but the punctilio of an honor the most sensitive, is then the standard of behavior.... the level of conduct for fiduciaries [has] been kept at a level higher than that trodden by the crowd.*
> Meinhard v. Salmon, *249 NY 461, 464 (1928).*

The language of fiduciary duty is stern and demanding—and so are the responsibilities it entails. The duties owed by fiduciaries include most importantly *loyalty, honesty*, and *candor*. The standard description is that a lawyer owes his or her client the duty of "utmost good faith and devotion." A good example of the duties of loyalty, honesty, and candor all at work at the same time is the requirement that a lawyer inform the client if the lawyer makes a material mistake in the representation, even if the lawyer might get fired and sued and even if the client is unlikely ever to discover it.

Note that a fiduciary also owes duties of competence and diligence. We discussed those in the previous chapter. Lawyers' failures with respect to competence and diligence usually receive separate treatment from other fiduciary duties, often under the label of "professional negligence," but the reason why a lawyer owes those duties to a particular client is that the lawyer is in a fiduciary relationship with the client.

Fidelity to the client in the Model Rules of Professional Conduct

Fidelity to the client is the foundation for several particular professional duties for lawyers under the rules of conduct. Many of the most significant rules are based upon the duty of fidelity to the client. In fact, these are the rules that that typically form the bulk of the law school course on professional responsibility. Those duties include:

- *Confidentiality—not disclosing information related to the representation of a client;*
- *Conflicts—avoiding interests that may prevent a lawyer from providing undivided loyalty to a client;*
- *Communication—keeping the client informed and making sure clients have adequate information to make informed decisions;*
- *Counseling—offering independent professional judgment and candid advice and counsel to clients;*
- *Client property and fees—protecting and keeping client property separate from that of the lawyer, and not charging or collecting fees that are unreasonable.*

Confidentiality

Model Rule of Professional Conduct 1.6 provides that a lawyer generally must keep confidential all information related to the representation of a client. That definition of confidential information is quite broad. "All information related to the representation" includes far more than statements that the client makes directly to the lawyer. It is broader than the attorney-client privilege. Anything the lawyer learns while representing a client that is not already widely known by the public must be kept confidential. A client may authorize a lawyer to reveal confidential information, but only after the lawyer has fully explained the risks of revealing and the alternatives to disclosure.

The duty to keep client information confidential extends to more than current clients of the lawyer. Rule 1.9(c) extends the same protection to former clients, and Rule 1.18 does so with respect to prospective clients. In fact, the duty to protect confidential information extends even beyond the death of the client, the former client, and the prospective client.

Rule 1.6(b) contains certain exceptions to the duty of confidentiality, circumstances under which the lawyer may reveal confidential information without the client's consent. It is important to note, however, that those exceptions never require a lawyer to reveal information, and disclosure is strictly limited to the extent necessary to meet the exception. Rule 1.13 also permits certain disclosures in the context of representing an entity. A lawyer must reveal confidential information in only two circumstances: when it is necessary to fulfill the lawyer's duty of candor to the court and when it is necessary to avoid assisting in a client's criminal or fraudulent conduct. Both of these situations implicate the lawyer's superseding duty of fidelity to the law, which we discuss in the next chapter.

Loyalty—avoiding conflicts of interest

Loyalty to the client includes avoiding any conflict that might impair the lawyer's ability to fully represent a client. There are numerous Model Rules related to conflicts of interest. Of particular note are Rule 1.7 (current client conflicts), Rule 1.8 (particular types of lawyer-client conflicts), Rule 1.9 (former client conflicts), and Rule 1.11 (conflicts of former government lawyers). The most general rule on conflicts, Rule 1.7, requires that lawyers decline representation when the interests of one client of the lawyer are directly adverse to another client of the lawyer. But prohibited conflicts go far beyond that. The rule requires lawyers to imagine and anticipate the risk of a conflict developing. A lawyer has a conflict of interest whenever there is a significant risk that anything else (responsibilities to current clients, to former clients, to third parties, or the lawyer's personal interests) will "materially limit" the lawyer's representation of any client.

Communication

Regular and candid communication with the client is an essential part of fidelity. Rule 1.4 requires the lawyer to keep the client informed, respond to requests for information, and make sure the client has enough information to make decisions. Failing to communicate regularly and adequately with clients leads to more disciplinary complaints against lawyers than any other factor. Clients are understandably unhappy when they are kept in the dark. It is not enough for the lawyer to be competent and on top of the case. Fidelity to the client requires lawyers to keep the client informed.

The duty of communication also includes the duty to reasonably consult with the client about the means of achieving the client's objectives. Clients have the authority to determine the goals of the representation, and many lawyers assume that, conversely, decisions about the means of achieving those objectives belong exclusively in the expert hands of the lawyer. That is incorrect. How to go about achieving client objectives is a shared responsibility between lawyer and client, and part of the lawyer's responsibility is to reasonably consult with the client about means.

Counseling and advice

A fundamental aspect of client loyalty is wise counsel and good advice. Clients usually come to lawyers when they are unable to solve problems on their own. Lawyers owe it to their clients under Rule 2.1 to offer independent professional judgment and candid advice.

Independent professional judgment is for the purpose of helping the client make decisions; it is emphatically not for the purpose of telling the client what to do. The client gets to decide what the client wants, and the client determines what is in his or her best interest. Clients have the exclusive authority to decide certain things, including the objectives of the representation, whether to plead guilty, and whether to settle a civil case. But your duty of fidelity to the client will include the duty to give your best advice.

A lawyer's counsel need not just be about technical legal matters. Under Rule 2.1, it is entirely appropriate, and sometimes necessary, to refer to non-legal considerations such as "moral, economic, social and political factors, that may be relevant to the client's situation." Most clients come to lawyers with problems that have many dimensions, including personal and moral factors. Some students express reluctance to discuss such matters with clients, in words such as "I am not a family therapist or a priest." That is true, but fidelity to the client will require you to help the client make the best decision for that client. Good counseling requires that you make sure that the client has reflected on *everything that matters to the client*, including both "legal" and "non-legal" issues.

The duty to counsel and advise sometimes includes the unpleasant duty to deliver bad news. The client may be facing a long prison term, or the likelihood of a substantial recovery in a civil case may turn out to be low. Whatever the bad news might be, the clients are entitled to know, and it will be your duty to tell them. You should do so in the kindest way possible, but fidelity to the client demands that you not shrink from telling the client the truth.

We have had students express the fear that as an agent of clients they will be required to do things that violate their own deeply held convictions. Let us speak some comfort to you if you have that fear. Lawyers owe their clients fidelity, utmost good faith, and devotion, but there are limits to the lawyer's obligation to follow a client's orders. First, you must refuse to help a client commit a crime or perpetrate a fraud. Second, except with respect to court appointments, you will have no obligation to undertake to represent any particular client. You get to decide what people or causes are worthy of your efforts. Third, even if you have already undertaken to represent a client, you may seek to withdraw under Rule 1.16(b)(4) if the client makes a decision with which you have a "fundamental disagreement" or the client insists on a course of action—even a perfectly legal one—that you find to be "repugnant." You will be an agent of your clients, but you will have choices, and you should not think of yourself as a "hired gun."

Fees and client property

As a lawyer, you will be entitled to be paid for your work, but you may not take advantage of your position and charge or collect from a client any fee that is not reasonable. Rule 1.5(a) sets forth criteria for determining whether a lawyer's fee is reasonable. It is crucial to realize that "the client agreed to it" is not the end of the matter. The amount of the fee is not simply a matter of negotiation between a lawyer and a client. Because the lawyer is in a position of trust, the rules require your fee to be objectively reasonable. Moreover, there are specific rules that restrict the fees that you will be able to charge in particular cases. For example, you will not be able to charge contingency fees in criminal or divorce cases, and you will not be permitted to accept payment from a third party without the informed consent of a client.

Reflecting the importance of lawyers as fiduciaries, Rule 1.15 is quite strict regarding the handling of client property. A lawyer may never co-mingle funds belonging to the client with funds belonging to the lawyer. And a lawyer must promptly deliver to the client any funds or other property that the client is entitled to receive. Upon request by the client, the lawyer also must promptly render a full accounting regarding the property.

WHAT CAUSES LAWYERS NOT TO DISPLAY FIDELITY TO THE CLIENT?

The ability to cheat on legal fees

One of the biggest challenges to your fidelity to the client will be money. In many types of private practice, you will be in a position where you can take advantage of your clients financially, often in situations where your actions will be undetectable.

Suppose you are billing the client at an agreed-upon hourly rate. Hourly billing is the most common way for lawyers in private practice to be paid. Suppose further that the rate itself is reasonable given the amount of skill required and the prevailing market rates in your community. There are numerous ways for you to cheat your client. You could bill for some time that you did not actually work—so-called "phantom billing." As long as you do not get carried away, who's going to know the difference? The client isn't watching you every minute. Or maybe you decide to work more hours on a file than is really necessary. You "work the file" or "churn the file," but not enough to be noticeable. You might also engage in the practice of "rounding up" your hours generously, such as having a "minimum" charge of a quarter hour even for tasks that take mere seconds like leaving a voicemail. The money is there for the taking, and lawyers are human. Temptation is ever present.

Note that your temptation to cheat on hours in the early stages of your career might be financial but indirect. If you are working in a firm, the partners will get the benefit of your cheating, but so will you. You can inflate your billable hours and impress the partners with your fake diligence. Some firms place great emphasis on the associates' billable hours. In the long run, you might believe, this will benefit you by way of a year-end bonus or an offer of partnership. It also gets easier every time you do it.

Temptation to take advantage of clients financially is not limited to hourly-rate lawyers. Suppose you are working on a personal injury case on a contingent fee. You receive a settlement offer that is less than the case is worth, but you know that the effort you will have to put into the case to get the client what the client deserves is disproportionate to the increase in the contingent fee you will earn. Or maybe you're a little short on cash that month. If all you care about is money, then you will be tempted to advise the client to take the settlement offer, pocket the fee, and move on to the next case. Most clients will take your advice when you advise them to settle. In the extreme, you could adopt a business model—often called a "settlement mill"—in which you advertise heavily, take in as many cases as possible, and settle them for whatever you can get quickly, regardless of the true value of the cases. A high volume of small contingent fees adds up and serves your financial interests, albeit at the cost of fidelity to the client.

Even in matters in which you have charged a flat rate or charged no fee at all there will be temptations to cheat. After all, with a flat rate paid up front (as in most criminal defense matters in private practice), you have no immediate economic incentive to go the extra mile out of fidelity to your client's interests. And a part of you may be inclined to think that a pro bono client has even less claim on your time. Flat-rate clients and pro bono clients have no way to assess your efforts. What you have to remember, of course, is that your duty of fidelity is exactly the same, regardless of how you are being paid and even if you are not being paid at all.

It is worth emphasizing that an important reason why legal fees will present a challenge to your fidelity to the client is that you will be able to tell yourself that you can get away with over-billing clients. Punishment for lawyers who charge unreasonable fees or who otherwise overbill their clients is exceedingly rare, primarily because it is so hard to detect. The ability to get away with unprofessional conduct exacerbates the risk.

Extreme financial pressures

The temptation to cheat your client on legal fees will be present regardless of whether you find yourself under any pressing financial need. But if you add to the mix a desperate need for money, then the likelihood of betraying the client's interests rises dramatically.

The typical way financial need will lead to a breach of fidelity to the client is when a lawyer perceives a short-term financial crunch. Perhaps the office rent is due, or it's time for a child's college tuition payment. A spouse may need urgent medical treatment. Lawyers who maintain trust accounts have ready access to other people's money. Many lawyers have breached their duty of fidelity to the client by "borrowing" funds from the trust account with the scrupulous promise to themselves that they will pay it back the next week when a client's settlement is finalized, or a slow-pay client finally pays the bill. The next week comes around, and the money has not come in. Another short-term "loan" from the trust account is necessary. And so it goes, with each dip into the trust account becoming easier until the lawyer may not even notice anymore that he is breaching a fundamental duty of fidelity (and one that will be easy for the bar to prove).

Mental illness and substance use

As we have noted, mental illness and substance use are significant problems in the legal profession. A lawyer in the midst of a major depressive episode is unlikely to display fidelity to the client. Client matters are neglected, and the lawyer feels compelled to lie about their status. You can often observe the same pattern in cases of addiction, where the lawyer's time and attention are devoted to obtaining and using his or her drug of choice. In those cases, the lawyer also commonly dips into the trust account to fund the addiction or to keep up with expenses. Lawyers who are dealing with mental illness or addiction are extremely likely to fail in their duties of fidelity to the client.

Pandering to a third-party payor rather than the client

When the lawyer's fee is paid by someone other than the client, there is a temptation for the lawyer to please the person who is paying the fee. Rule 1.8(f) is clear that, while it can be permissible for someone other than the client to pay the attorney, it is only permissible when the client gives informed consent, the lawyer keeps all communications with the client confidential, and the person paying the lawyer does not interfere with the lawyer's independent professional judgment in serving the client. Despite this rule, it can be all too easy to want to please the person paying the fee or to reveal confidential information to that person or allow the person paying the fee to call the shots. For example, a parent who pays a child's legal fees for a divorce might feel entitled to know what's going on and weigh in on how the matter should proceed. That's inconsistent with the lawyer's duties of fidelity to the client. When someone other than the client is paying the fee, lawyers must be especially vigilant to protect the client's interest and to make clear to the payor that the lawyer may not reveal confidential information or take direction from anyone other than the client.

The most common example of lawyers being paid by someone other than the client is in insurance defense. Even when an insurance company has selected the lawyer to handle the case and is paying for the defense of its insured, the insured person is the lawyer's client to whom the lawyer owes fidelity. It can be all too tempting for the lawyer to forget who is the client, especially since insurance defense lawyers tend to be retained repeatedly by the same insurance companies, while the lawyer is unlikely ever to represent the insured again. This can cause the lawyer to fail to communicate with the insured client, or to give more weight or pay more attention to the insurance adjuster's views than the client's.

Fear

There are things to be afraid of in the practice of law. One situation in which fear often causes a lawyer to breach the duty of fidelity to the client is when the lawyer makes a mistake. As we noted, a lawyer who makes a material mistake is obliged to inform the client. Rule 1.4 and the fiduciary duties of loyalty and candor demand it. The client is entitled to know of the mistake, if for no other reason to decide whether to allow the lawyer to continue the representation. Yet many lawyers rationalize not doing so. They fear the embarrassment, and they fear losing the client. Those fears lead to a breach of the duty of fidelity to the client.

Special considerations in representing individuals

Some of the challenges you will face to your fidelity to the client will be a function of the practice setting you choose. There are over 1.3 million lawyers in the United States, and they work in a wide range of office settings. About 75% work in private practice, 10–12% work full time for the government, and 8–10% work for private organizations as in-house counsel. About 22% of lawyers in private practice work in firms of 6–100 lawyers, while about 16% of all private practitioners work in large firms of more than 100 lawyers (American Bar Foundation 2011). Lawyers in mid-size and large firms generally represent organizations; they rarely represent individuals, other than the very wealthiest persons.

About 60% of all lawyers in private practice work in offices of 1–5 lawyers. These sole and small firm practitioners often represent individual clients in what been labeled "personal plight" areas of the law (Heinz and Laumann 1978, 1126). These include matters such as divorce, criminal law, personal injury, immigration, landlord-tenant, and consumer litigation, including bankruptcy. Public defenders who represent indigent criminal defendants and legal aid lawyers who represent the poor in civil matters also fall within the definition of "personal plight" lawyers.

Representing people rather than organizations may bring you some of your greatest joy as a lawyer. It is easier to sense that you have made a difference when the client is a person. But representing people brings some special challenges to your fidelity to the client. They come to you at times of crisis, when the stakes are high and they desperately need help. They are highly likely to be stressed by the situation but inexperienced in dealing with the law or with lawyers. They may be needy and demand a disproportionate (to you) amount of your time and attention.

Your duty of fidelity to the client remains the same, but you will be struggling with a powerful constraint: time. In private practice, the business model for most lawyers who represent people requires volume. No one client can pay the rent, but a high volume of clients with swift rates of turnover can create a profitable practice. You will find yourself stretched when you try to give individualized attention to every client. Similarly, public defender and civil legal services offices tend to be extremely underfunded, with the result that the lawyers have high caseloads and precious little time to devote to any one client.

You also may find that some of your individual clients are, to put it mildly, not at their best. Clients who are undergoing marital breakup, are in serious debt, have lost their job, or have been injured, and those who are facing imprisonment, deportation, or eviction, are going through very difficult times. It's not surprising that people facing such difficult and stressful events can be highly emotional and difficult to deal with. They can also be quite demanding that the lawyer "fix" the problem. These reactions by clients are normal and understandable. From the lawyer's standpoint, however, especially in a very busy practice, these clients can seem unreasonable or unpleasant.

Not surprisingly, lawyers who are pressed for time and think of clients as "unpleasant" or "unreasonable" are less likely to exhibit fidelity to those clients. You may feel tempted to ignore the client's repeated requests for information, or to take the actions you believe best (after all, you're the lawyer) without consulting with your client or following the client's instructions. These are breaches of the duty of fidelity to the client. It is unsurprising that most disciplinary complaints against lawyers arise from failures to communicate promptly with clients or that a sizable majority of such complaints against lawyers are filed by clients in "personal plight" areas of the law such as family law, personal injury, and criminal defense.

Special considerations in representing organizations

When a law firm represents organizations such as corporations rather than individuals, there are different challenges to maintaining fidelity to the client. It is easy for the lawyer to forget that the entity is the client, and it can be tempting to be less vigilant about conflicts of interest. Lawyers who serve as in-house counsel have special challenges.

Lawyers for entities owe the same duty of loyalty as to any other client, including the duties to keep confidences, to avoid conflicts of interest, to communicate fully, and to provide independent counsel. Rule 1.13 of the Model Rules is clear that when a lawyer represents an organization, the *organization* is the client. But in representing an entity such as a corporation, the lawyer necessarily communicates with and counsels the actual human beings who are officers, directors, and employees of the organization. Unlike individual clients in "personal plight" cases, businesses (especially the larger businesses that are the principal clients of larger law firms) tend to need lawyers on a regular basis. Lawyers who represent those businesses develop close working relationships with the individuals in management. The problem comes when the lawyer begins to think of those individuals as clients, and thereby fails to recognize the managers of the business can have interests, and sometimes take actions, that conflict with the interests of the entity. Model Rule 1.13(b) requires the lawyer to take appropriate action to protect the entity from the managers, but the lawyer may find it hard to do so when the managers are the ones with whom the lawyer deals and who have the power to fire the firm. The lawyer can exercise fidelity to the client only if the lawyer clearly recognizes the identity and interests of the entity client and is prepared to risk the consequences of protecting the entity.

Although all lawyers must avoid conflicts of interest, there are special problems in large firms in how they treat conflicts. The more lawyers there are in a firm, the more clients the firm is likely to have. The more clients a firm has, the more likely it is that a new matter will create a conflict for the firm. Under Rule 1.10(a), most conflicts of any one lawyer will be imputed to all the lawyers in the firm, even if the firm has hundreds of lawyers and offices all over the world. Potential conflicts abound for large firms. If a firm declines a new matter or a new client because of a conflict, the result is loss of that new business and perhaps strife and turmoil within the firm. Both of these consequences may lead the firm's leaders to allow their judgment to be clouded, with the result that the firm places itself in a position where its duty of loyalty will be compromised.

If you practice as in-house counsel for a corporation or another organization, you will have a particularly acute problem: your one client will also be your employer. Your boss, or some other powerful person in the firm, may take action that harms the company. Your job is to protect the company, but if you do so you might lose your job. The duties of fidelity to the client are no different for lawyers who have only one client, but fulfilling those duties may be harder.

Self-interests other than money interfering with fidelity to the client

Not all self-interest that can interfere with fidelity to the client is "selfish" in the narrow sense. You need to be aware any time that an interest of yours may interfere with full loyalty to your clients.

One example is your own sense of what is right and wrong, or wise and unwise. A client may propose a perfectly legal course of action with which you strongly disagree. Your job is to give advice. The client gets to decide. Most clients will take your advice, but some will not. At that point, your job is to help the client unless you are prepared to withdraw because you find the course of action "repugnant" or you have a "fundamental disagreement" with it. If you proceed, your duties of fidelity are just the same whether you agree with what you have been instructed to do or not. You must provide the full loyalty that the client deserves. Being judgmental about the client's decision will not help.

Another example is when you are representing a client but also have a cause that you care about. Maybe you have filed a suit for a client and intend to use the case to advance the cause. Your duties of fidelity run to the client, not to the cause. You may be tempted to use the client in service to the cause, but you must be prepared to forego that chance, no matter how noble the cause. As long as you are the lawyer, you must use that position of trust and power for the benefit of the client even if it hurts your cause.

STRATEGIES FOR CULTIVATING A PROFESSIONAL IDENTITY THAT INCLUDES A DISPOSITION TOWARD FIDELITY TO THE CLIENT

There are steps you can begin to take now that will help you acquire, cultivate, and deploy a professional identity that includes fidelity to the client as one of its virtues.

Cultivate a fiduciary disposition of putting others first

As we have seen, the language of fiduciary duty is demanding: utmost good faith, selfless devotion, scrupulous honesty, and so on. Understanding these obligations is essential. But complying with them in practice will require more than understanding; it will require an inner commitment. Practicing with fidelity to the client requires you to cultivate what has been called a fiduciary disposition (Hamilton 2017). A fiduciary disposition is a commitment to serve the interest of another rather than yourself. As a lawyer, a fiduciary disposition leads to your reflexively thinking first about your client's interests, even when they are at odds with your self-interest.

Having a true fiduciary disposition may be particularly challenging for law students and young lawyers who, up until the beginning of their professional careers, have likely only been in situations in which they alone suffer from a failure to act competently or diligently. For example, you may be accustomed to making decisions about the costs of failures of diligence when only you will suffer the consequences; it takes some practice to fully develop an understanding that the calculation is different when someone else will pay the price. In law school, even before you have clients, you should begin to lay the groundwork for this fiduciary disposition. In working out hypothetical problems in your classes, be mindful that getting to the right answer is not just about the grade you will receive, or the reaction from your peers or your professor, but it will also affect the client who is counting on you. That may be a hypothetical client for the moment, but soon enough it will be a real person or entity who will be affected by your failure to prepare thoroughly to bring all of your skills to bear on a problem.

A fiduciary disposition requires more than just putting the client first; you must also do your best to understand a client from the client's point of view. It requires that you exhibit *empathy* toward your clients. Empathy is the setting aside of ourselves in order to understand another. Empathy doesn't come naturally or easily, at least not most of the time, but it is a skill that can be cultivated. Empathy is not the same as sympathy, nor is it a feeling of affection toward the client. A fiduciary disposition doesn't require you to like your client, and you need not agree with choices they have made or with a course of action they want to take. It does require that you genuinely try to understand your client from your client's point of view, including the client's priorities, motivations, fears, concerns, and desires.

True empathy is difficult for anyone, but this kind of openness and understanding of the other can be *particularly* difficult for lawyers. Here's why:

- *We need to overcome our training that has conditioned us to evaluate, to judge, to make counter-arguments; what lawyers may think of as "listening" is often simply preparing their response.*
- *We need to be open to more than the legally relevant. Lawyers are trained in law school to separate the relevant from the irrelevant, to spot the issues and ignore everything else. Much of what the client says would be irrelevant if the problem was a law school examination—and yet much of this legally "irrelevant" information is crucial to providing effective representation. The client's feelings, motivations, relationships, and priorities can be even more important than the historical events that constitute the legally relevant facts.*
- *We need to set aside our competitive instincts. You may have the urge to argue with a client, or to "one-up" the client's knowledge or experiences. This may happen without any awareness on your part—but the client may feel it acutely.*
- *We must see each client as a unique individual. Experienced lawyers may believe that they have seen it all, that they don't have anything to learn from a particular client, or that all clients in particular kinds of cases are alike (e.g., "you've seen one child custody dispute you've seen them all"; or, "I know what an injured client needs without asking"). Assumptions such as these obviously impair real empathy with individual clients.*

We can overcome these occupational hazards, and we must. A fiduciary disposition is always infused with empathy.

In addition to developing empathy, you must also learn the skill of setting boundaries so that you do not become absorbed in all the client's problems or get sucked into any dysfunction. Setting appropriate boundaries protects your own well-being, but it also helps you deliver the professional detachment and independent advice that clients deserve. Empathy and appropriate boundaries may seem mutually exclusive; in fact, they are both necessary in a helping relationship, and they can be mutually reinforcing. Lawyers can learn from other professions such as therapy, social work, and pastoral counseling, which place great emphasis in their training on how to set appropriate boundaries.

Moreover, empathy will open you up to how your representation of the client is experienced by the client, which will strengthen your fiduciary disposition. You will be less likely to take advantage of your position of trust because you appreciate the client's vulnerability. You will be more willing to undertake the hard work to develop competence and to act with diligence. You will be motivated to keep the client informed and to provide wise counseling and advice because you understand the stakes for your client. Your starting point will be to act with the required good faith and attention to your client's interests because you feel deeply how much the client needs you and appreciate fully the consequences of letting the client down.

Financial expectations and prudence

As you have seen, money gets in the way of fidelity to the client as much as, or more than, any other factor. One way to reduce the negative impact of money on fidelity to the client is to become more realistic and self-aware about personal finances. Money can become an issue when the lawyer wants more (financial expectations) or needs more (often, but not always, as a result of financial imprudence). Law students and lawyers should have realistic expectations about the money they will make. Such expectations can act as a brake on the drive to meet an artificial target. Research now the likely income you will have in the type of practice you wish to have. Budget accordingly. A habit of budgeting and living below one's means can also reduce the pressure to betray a client for financial reasons.

We discussed above the most egregious cases of lawyer self-dealing, such as "borrowing" from the client trust account. The vast majority of lawyers do not engage in such conduct, and the few lawyers who do so would tell you that they did not expect to become that kind of lawyer. Sometimes financial calamity happens for reasons beyond your control, but too many lawyers spent or borrowed their way into situations in which the only way out seemed to be to use client money. You can avoid their fate.

Remember the "internal goods" of the practice of law

We frankly set out for you earlier in this chapter various ways in which you could cheat your clients and stand a decent chance of getting away with it. You need not have much fear of punishment if you only steal a little at a time. But remember the lesson of modern virtue ethics: you can only obtain the "internal goods" of the practice of law—the deep satisfaction that comes with being a particular type of lawyer—by living up to the expectations of the practice. One of those expectations is that at all times you will act with fidelity to the client. It may seem ironic, but for your own sake you must be hyper-vigilant about acting selflessly for the benefit of others. You hurt the client and you harm yourself by becoming something less than you now aspire to be.

Be sensitive to organizational expectations and ethos

It is important to try to discover the ethos of any organization in which you might work. Not all firms or government offices are the same. Watch for clues to see if the firm acts with fidelity to the client in all ways.

For example, if you go to work in a firm that bills by the hour, reflect on the instructions you are given about billing a client. One of us in orientation at a now-defunct large firm was instructed, "if you would rather be doing something else, bill the time." The message that sends about clients and billing time is clear. Fortunately, that type of attitude toward billing is not universal. Another of us remembers well the orientation lecture at a different law firm on hourly billing by the senior partner in the firm. He told us that billing clients by the hour was a privilege that must not be abused. We should take the viewpoint that clients have opened their checkbooks to their lawyers, allowing us to write checks to ourselves from the client's account. He suggested that we imagine that the client is literally in the room watching you work; don't bill the time unless you would be comfortable with the client paying for that time. These very different approaches to billing reflect the fundamentally different organizational ethos of those two firms. Firm culture matters. New lawyers may be particularly impressionable, and if they see cheating they may come to believe that it is an accepted part of being in the legal profession.

The same powers of intentional observation will serve you well in other types of practices. In a personal injury practice, take note when the firm's need for cash creeps into the decision about whether to settle a case. If you are in a public defender's office, observe how much time lawyers are able to give to each client. In each instance, reflect on the duties of fidelity to the clients. If you are working in an insurance defense firm, watch for signs that the client's interests are secondary to the insurance company's interests.

The basic lesson is this: when you show up for work that first day, remember everything you know about fidelity to the client. Then continuously compare what you know with what you are seeing.

Cultivate self-awareness

Before you can do anything about a situation in which your loyalties might be tested, you must be aware of the temptations to favor your self-interest over that of your client. Are you not returning a phone call because the client is difficult and too demanding? Are you interpreting the conflict of interest rules narrowly in order to obtain new business or avoid a fight within the firm? How much is your work driven by the need to hit a billable hour quota? These questions, and dozens of others, should echo in your mind as you strive to act with fidelity to your clients.

It is easy to rationalize self-interested behavior. In fact, sometimes rationalization keeps us from seeing the conflict between self and client at all. Other times, we recognize the conflict, but we convince ourselves that we can satisfy self and client without any sacrifice.

Rationalizing self-interested behavior is a universal human phenomenon, but we lawyers, who are trained in argument, are especially prone. We need to stop and think about our motivations and be brutally honest with ourselves. Any time you suspect that something is not above board, it is especially critical to stop and reflect. Don't ignore that nagging feeling that something isn't quite right; that feeling is an excellent prompt for further reflection. This reflection can take several forms.

We have all heard the cliché that "I have to be able to look myself in the mirror." That phrase may have originated with an ambassador who resigned from service rather than organize a dinner at which King Edward VII expected prostitutes. The ambassador said, "I refuse to see a pimp in the mirror in the morning when I shave." Other versions include "I wonder what my Mother would say if she knew" and "how would this look on the front page of the New York Times tomorrow." Regardless of the mantra, the point is to stop, think, and consider rather than just go along under suspicious circumstances.

Imagine what a moral exemplar would do

If your judgment remains clouded, or if your nerve to act against self-interest begins to fail, imagine what a moral exemplar would do. It often takes courage to do what is contrary to our own self-interest, such as turning down a lucrative new client because of a conflict of interest with a current client. Sometimes lawyers must even face the hostility of others. It took courage for John Adams to represent the British soldiers accused of firing on unarmed persons in the Boston Massacre. It took courage for Thurgood Marshall to travel the backroads of the South and appear before hostile court-rooms in the effort to desegregate the schools. The point is, in remembering that Adams or Marshall could be faithful to their clients in the face of threats and worse, you may find the courage to face up to the pressures to betray your client.

Reminders help. You may even now keep things around you that evoke thoughts of people you desire to emulate. Maybe you keep a picture of a parent, or a favorite teacher, in a place where it reminds you of that resolve. Lawyers do similar things to remind them of how they aspire to conduct themselves as lawyers. Many keep pictures or other reminders in their offices of the people whose character and courage they admire. It might be Bryan Stevenson or Clarence Darrow, or a beloved mentor or friend, but when logic fails the imagination can take over. If, in a moment of crisis, you can discern that your moral exemplar would choose a particular course of action, then that will tell you something about what you should do.

CONCLUSION

Fidelity to the client is an essential component of a lawyer's professional identity. Such fidelity includes confidentiality, loyalty, communication, counseling, and utmost good faith. Many interests, especially self-interests, can come between a lawyer and a client, but the lawyer is expected to have the self-awareness and discipline to see those interests and overcome them. Selfless service to another brings many of the deepest joys of the practice of law. You want your work to matter to others, and it will, when you act with fidelity to your clients.

DISCUSSION QUESTIONS AND PROBLEMS

1 As we have seen, personal problems and substance use often inhibit lawyers' ability to provide the representation that clients deserve. Reflect on the habits you have as a student and the habits you plan to cultivate as a lawyer to remain at your best. Specifically address habits of health and wellness, which may include exercise, diet, rest and recreation, and mindfulness and other spiritual practices.

2   Similarly, financial pressures often interfere with lawyers' fidelity to their clients. Reflect upon your current and future financial habits and practices. How do you define financial success and how important is that to you?

3   In order to understand the pressures involved in hourly billing, try keeping your time spent on your law school work for a couple of weeks. How contemporaneously did you record your time? Hourly, daily, weekly? How did the frequency of your recording affect the accuracy of your timekeeping? What did you "count" as school work for this purpose? Did you feel the temptation to round up or estimate your time?

4   We emphasized empathy as a crucial part of cultivating a fiduciary disposition. While important for lawyers, empathy is also helpful in your personal and intimate relationships. Practice listening to a friend or loved one with the purpose of truly understanding what they are saying. As you listen, try to avoid judging them, or preparing your response, or pointing out how they are wrong, or letting your mind wander to something else, or jumping too quickly to assuring them that you understand them. You may find that it is harder than you expect to listen without doing any of these other things. You will also most certainly find, though, that this kind of empathetic listening will improve the relationship.

5   Have you ever had a situation in your life in which you have put the interests of someone else ahead of your own, perhaps a family member or a close friend? How did it feel to set aside your needs and wants, even temporarily, for the sake of someone else?

6   You will likely find in practice that you represent a client that you disagree with or simply do not like for one reason or another. You will nonetheless be required to put that client's interests ahead of your own. Think about situations in your life where you have had to relate to people you don't like or disagree with. How did you manage to work with them or relate to them? What does that tell you about how you may be able to be candid, loyal, and honest in representing such people?

REFERENCE LIST AND SUGGESTED READINGS

American Bar Foundation. 2011. *Data on the Legal Profession.* www.americanbar.org/content/dam/aba/migrated/marketresearch/PublicDocuments/lawyer_demographics_2011.authcheckdam.pdf.

American Law Institute. 2000. *Restatement of the Law (Third) of the Law Governing Lawyers.* St. Paul: American Law Institute Publishers.

"Fidelity." The New Shorter Oxford English Dictionary, Calvendon Press, Oxford, 1993, p. 942.

Hamilton, Neil W. 2017. Internalizing a Fiduciary Mindset to Put the Client First. *The Professional Lawyer* 24:3.

Heinz, John P., and Laumann, Edward O. 1978. The Legal Profession: Client Interests, Professional Roles, and Social Hierarchies. *Michigan Law Review* 76:1111.

Lerman, Lisa G. 1990. Lying to Clients. *University of Pennsylvania Law Review* 138:659.

Mather, Lynn. 2013. Lawyerly Fidelity: An Ethical and Empirical Critique. *Nomos — American Society for Political and Legal Philosophy* 54:106.

Miller, William R. 2018. *Listening Well: The Art of Empathetic Understanding.* Eugene: Wipf and Stock.

Nichols, Michael P. 2009. *The Lost Art of Listening: How Learning to Listen Can Improve Relationships.* New York: The Guilford Press.

Schiltz, Patrick J. 1999. On Being a Happy, Healthy, and Ethical Member of an Unhappy, Unhealthy, and Unethical Profession. *Vanderbilt Law Review* 52:871.

Semple, Noel. 2014. Personal Plight, Legal Practice, and Tomorrow's Lawyers. *Journal of the Legal Profession* 39:25.

Silver, Marjorie. 2007. *The Affective Assistance of Counsel.* Durham: Carolina Academic Press.

5

FIDELITY TO LAW
AS A PROFESSIONAL VIRTUE

INTRODUCTION

The next of the six virtues of the lawyer's professional identity is fidelity to the law. You're not going to easily find fidelity to the law set out in a single rule of any code of professional responsibility or statute. Nor are you going to find case law that punishes something called a lack of fidelity to the law. Yet the expectation that lawyers will follow the law permeates rules of conduct, professionalism creeds and case law. A good example is the Preamble to the Model Rules, which provides that:

> A lawyer's conduct should conform to the requirements of the law, both in professional service to clients and in the lawyer's business and personal affairs. A lawyer should use the law's procedures only for legitimate purposes and not to harass or intimidate others. A lawyer should demonstrate respect for the legal system and for those who serve it, including judges, other lawyers and public officials. While it is a lawyer's duty, when necessary, to challenge the rectitude of official action, it is also a lawyer's duty to uphold legal process.

There can be no doubt that one of the virtues you need to cultivate and deploy as a professional lawyer is fidelity to the law.

From one perspective, this may seem an odd thing to include on a short list of lawyerly virtues, as all citizens have an obligation to abide by the law. In fact, the criminal and civil justice systems are built around this expectation. There are, however, several reasons why fidelity to the law must be central to the lawyer's professional identity. First, lawyers are in many ways the embodiment of the law. Their professional time and talent are spent in helping others navigate its complexities, ensure compliance with it, and deal with the consequences when it is not followed. Sources of professional ethics guidance, including rules of professional conduct and professionalism creeds, recognize—in varying language—this critical reality: the law is at the heart of a lawyer's role, and therefore the lawyer has a special obligation to follow, uphold, and advance the law. As the Preamble states, the lawyer is "an officer of the legal system," implying that the lawyer's role includes compliance with and enforcement of the law. It is a well-accepted affirmative obligation that the good lawyer acts consistently with the law.

But there is also another reason. The lawyer's obligation of fidelity to the client, and the fact that lawyers operate in an adversary system, mean that fulfilling the virtue of fidelity to the law can be especially challenging. Deborah Rhode is one of the leading scholars on legal ethics and has written, "[t]he clash between lawyers' responsibilities as officers of the court and advocates of client interests creates the most fundamental dilemmas of legal ethics" (Rhode 2000, 50). The duty of fidelity to the law serves as a constraint on over-commitment to fidelity to the client, which may lead the lawyer into situations where failure to follow the law seems like the good, or even the only, way to act. Doing so is especially tempting when the lawyer becomes so committed to a cause or to a client that the lawyer is able to rationalize violating the law. Lawyers have lost their way by hiding evidence or facilitating perjury because the failure to do so was likely to result in defeat.

Being faithful to the law is complex for other reasons as well. First, the law is not always clear. You are spending much of your legal education learning how to make legal arguments on both sides of legal questions. How can you be faithful to the law when it is not always clear what the law is? Yet you must. We also know that various laws can be in tension with each other. As you are learning, the United States Supreme Court has frequently struck down state laws because they violate constitutional guarantees. Even a clear law can be, or argued to be, invalid.

Another complexity is that fidelity to the law does not mean that you must accept unjust or unwise laws or judicial decisions. This freedom to challenge the status quo can at first seem to be at odds with a requirement to be faithful to the law. It is not—the ability of the lawyer to work within the law to change the law is part of the genius of our system. In fact, part of the virtue of public spiritedness (which we will discuss in detail in the next chapter) is to work to improve the law. American history is replete with example of lawyers who have effected great changes because of their willingness to challenge law or to argue for it to adapt to new realities of technological, scientific or social change. Laws that supported segregation were eliminated because passionate, committed, and talented lawyers challenged them. The law of evidence changed in response to scientific advances such as DNA. We could list dozens of examples.

This chapter will offer some guidance on how the lawyer navigates these complexities while fulfilling the virtue of fidelity to the law. We will elaborate on particular aspects of fidelity to the law and discuss the most common challenges to doing so. We will offer suggestions for overcoming those challenges. As with the other virtues, we will emphasize the need to internalize a personal commitment to fidelity to the law because external constraints are not enough to ensure that lawyers will conduct themselves as they should.

WHAT DOES "FIDELITY TO THE LAW" MEAN?

Fidelity to the law is a broad concept. The law that governs your conduct as a lawyer is pervasive and complex. There are rules, statutes, judicial decisions, and constitutional provisions to which a lawyer must be faithful. Because we cannot explore every law, case, or rule to which you must show fidelity, we are going to discuss some carefully chosen particular examples. Unsurprisingly, many (but not all) of these specific applications of the general duty arise in the context of the lawyer's role as an advocate.

The duty to assert only meritorious claims and contentions

The Model Rules recognize that the lawyer's role as advocate requires that the lawyer be a gatekeeper to the courts. This means that lawyers shall not advance claims or defenses that lack merit or take

any actions to advance positions that are not justified by the law or facts. Model Rul
lawyers may not

> bring or defend a proceeding, or assert or controvert an issue therein, un!_
> in law and fact for doing so that is not frivolous, which includes a good faith argui...
> extension, modification or reversal of existing law.

You may not invoke the processes of the judicial system unless there a legitimate reason for doing so. The fact that it might be in the client's strategic interest to bring a frivolous claim or make a frivolous argument is irrelevant—your duty of fidelity to the law forbids you to help your client that way.

It is important to note two special aspects of the lawyer's role as gatekeeper. First, as we have said before, the lawyer is free to challenge the status quo as long as the challenge is not frivolous. Also, Rule 3.1 contains a special exception for criminal defense attorneys, who are allowed to insist that the prosecution meet its responsibility to prove a case against the defendant by proof beyond a reasonable doubt. It is not improper for a lawyer to bring a not guilty plea and to put the state to its obligation to prove its case, even if the lawyer knows that the defendant committed the alleged crimes and recognizes that the chance of an acquittal is low.

Generally, however, the lawyer is expected to keep the judicial pipeline clear of debris that should not be there. This duty is present in the Model Rules and is also echoed in court rules, including Federal Rule of Civil Procedure 11 and the Rules of Appellate Procedure. There are a number of cases in which courts have imposed sanctions under these rules upon attorneys for making claims that were unsupported by the law (or a good faith argument to change the law) or the facts. Being a faithful gatekeeper is part of your duty of fidelity to the law.

The duty to expedite litigation

Similarly, the rules require the lawyer to respect the litigation process and to fulfill the role of officer of the court by expediting litigation. In practice, this means that the lawyer must not act improperly to delay the judicial process, even if delay may benefit the lawyer's client. Model Rule 3.2 requires lawyers to make reasonable efforts to expedite litigation "consistent with the interests of the client," but the comment to the rule provides that delay is improper "if done for the purpose of frustrating an opposing party's attempt to obtain rightful redress or repose ... [and] [r]ealizing financial or other benefit from otherwise improper delay in litigation is not a legitimate interest of the client." Again, fidelity to the law takes precedence over fidelity to the client.

This obligation is reinforced by statutes, rules, and case law that provide the courts with statutory or inherent authority to punish the lawyer who unnecessarily delays litigation. For example, 28 U.S.C. §1927 empowers federal courts to sanction a lawyer personally if the lawyer "multiplies the proceedings in any case unreasonably and vexatiously...." Under Federal Rule of Civil Procedure 37, a court may impose severe sanctions if a party does not comply with discovery obligations. And the Supreme Court of the United States held, in *Chambers v. Nasco*, 501 U.S. 32 (1991), that federal courts have the inherent power to sanction lawyers and parties who engage in bad-faith tactics to thwart the court's ability to provide effective relief to an opposing party. Fidelity to the law requires an attorney to allow proceedings to take their normal course even if it means that lawyer's client will suffer.

ne duty of candor

Model Rule 3.3 imposes several duties of candor to the courts. A lawyer may not make misrepresentations of fact or law to a court and, in certain rare circumstances (such as when a lawyer's client has died), the lawyer even has an affirmative obligation to reveal facts. Lawyers are not allowed to present evidence that they know is false, and if the lawyer presents evidence and later comes to know of its falsity, the lawyer must take steps that ultimately may include revealing the falsity of the evidence to the court. More generally, if a lawyer knows that anyone has perpetrated, is perpetrating, or intends to perpetrate a crime or a fraud related to a proceeding in which the lawyer is participating, the lawyer must act. All of these situations present obvious potential to conflict with the duty of fidelity to the client.

The practical challenges of navigating such situations have resulted in some of the most famous cases in legal ethics. One is Nix v.Whiteside, 475 U.S. 157 (1986). The defendant was on trial for murder and was asserting a claim of self-defense. After initially telling his lawyer that he had not seen a gun in the victim's hands, the defendant changed his story and wanted to testify that he had seen "something metallic" because if he didn't say that to the jury "he was dead." The lawyer told his client that if he testified that way the lawyer would tell the court that the testimony was false. The client testified but did not say that he had seen something metallic in the victim's hands. He was found guilty. The client then accused the lawyer of ineffective assistance of counsel. The Supreme Court of the United States found that the Sixth Amendment right to effective assistance of counsel does not include a right to the lawyer's cooperation in offering perjured testimony and that the lawyer had correctly balanced his duty of advocacy for the client with his duty of candor with the court. The Court held that the lawyer's threat to reveal client confidences to the court was appropriate and ethical because the duty of candor to the court overrode the duty of confidentiality to the client in this instance.

In another well-known case, Robert Bennett, a lawyer for former President Bill Clinton, submitted an affidavit from Monica Lewinsky during the President's deposition in an attempt to foreclose questions of the President about his relationship with Ms. Lewinsky. In the affidavit, Ms. Lewinsky stated falsely that "there was absolutely no sex of any kind in any manner, shape or form with the President." When Mr. Bennett later learned that this statement was false, he wrote a letter to the judge presiding over the case in which he described the affidavit as "misleading and not true" and that "pursuant to our professional responsibility, we wanted to advise you that the Court should not rely on Ms. Lewinsky's affidavit or remarks of counsel characterizing that affidavit…." This letter is now justly famous as an example of a lawyer's fulfilling his duty of candor to the court even though doing so harmed the lawyer's client.

The duty not to counsel or assist a witness to testify falsely

Related to the obligation of the lawyer to fulfill the duty of candor to the court is an independent requirement under Rule 3.4(b) related to the role of the advocate in preparing a witness. The rule forbids lawyers from counseling or assisting a witness to testify falsely. Advocates are expected to be zealous for their clients, but they can't cheat. Coaching a witness to lie is cheating.

Many law students have learned about this duty through a fictionalized account of a lawyer's careful (and perhaps improper) counseling of an astute client in preparation for giving testimony.

In the film *Anatomy of a Murder*, the lawyer engages in a colloquy with his client, who is charged with murder, in which he effectively coaches the client to give answers that will support the defense of insanity (*Anatomy of a Murder* 1959). Without first asking the client what happened, the lawyer gives the so-called "lawyer's lecture" and describes to the client each category of justification for murder and, one by one, rules out its applicability in this case. The lawyer keeps the client guessing about where he is going until the client says, "I must have been mad," to which the lawyer responds, "Sorry, bad temper isn't a defense." The client's response is "No, I must have been crazy." "Well," replies the lawyer, "see if you can remember how crazy you were." The client then either remembers or fabricates the facts to support the defense of insanity. The lawyer may have cheated by skillfully guiding his client to tell a potentially persuasive lie.

From the real world comes another illustration that has stirred much controversy. During the deposition of a plaintiff in an asbestosis case, a witness preparation memo used by the plaintiff's firm of Baron and Budd was inadvertently produced to the defendants' counsel. A recurrent issue in asbestos litigation is whether the plaintiff was harmed by the defendant's product or by the products of other companies. Among other guidance, the memo gave the following instructions to Baron & Budd clients (Biederman et al. 1998):

- *"Remember to say that you saw the names on the bags."*
- *"You may be asked how you can recall so many product names. The best answer is to say you recall seeing the names on the containers or on the products itself. The more you thought about it, the more you remembered!"*
- *"Do not say that you saw more or one brand or another, or that one brand was more commonly used than another … Be confident that you saw as much of one brand as all the others."*

This witness preparation form received much criticism when it came to light because, the critics claimed, it encouraged plaintiffs to give certain testimony without regard to whether it was true. That would be a clear violation of the lawyers' duty of fidelity to the law. That would be cheating. On the other hand, Baron and Budd defended the memo as effective witness preparation in the service of the lawyer's duty of advocacy, as an act of fidelity to the clients.

The duty not to assist with crimes or frauds

Model Rule 1.2(d) prohibits a lawyer from counseling or assisting a client in the perpetration of a crime or a fraud. A lawyer's guidance or assistance with such activity might well have real advantages for a client, including the use of methods that are less likely to be detected. Yet a lawyer's fidelity to the client does not extend this far and in fact collides with other law—the law of crimes and frauds—that is imported into this rule.

One instructive example on this point is the case of OPM Leasing Services, Inc. ("OPM" stands for "other people's money"). OPM's law firm helped it close numerous transactions that, apparently unbeknownst at first to its lawyers, were fraudulent. Supposedly, OPM was in the business of borrowing money to purchase computers that were then leased. The rents from these leases were to provide the funds to pay back the loans and also serve as collateral for the loans. But OPM obtained millions of dollars in loans based upon fictitious leases. Its lawyers helped it close these transactions.

OPM's president eventually confessed to the lawyers that the deals were frauds but promised that future deals would not be. After consulting with legal ethics experts (and perhaps double-checking the fact that OPM accounted for 60% of their business), the lawyers decided that they could continue to close loans for OPM. These, too, turned out to be fraudulent. If Rule 1.2(d) had been in effect at that time (it was not), and the lawyers knew that the new transactions were fraudulent (they claimed they did not), then this part of the OPM story would be a classic example of lawyers who violated their duties of fidelity to the law by helping a client perpetrate a fraud.

A lawyer who is asked to give impermissible assistance must refuse to give it but is permitted to advise the client not to engage in the activity and to explain the possible consequences of doing so. To that limited extent, the lawyer may act with fidelity to the client by dissuading the client from engaging in criminal or fraudulent conduct. It's usually good advice not to commit a crime or a fraud. But the ability to be faithful to the client's interests ends when the client rejects that advice and wants help with a criminal or fraudulent scheme. Then the lawyer's duty of fidelity to the client collides with the duty of fidelity to the law, and the duty to the law prevails.

The general duty not to unlawfully impede access to evidence

Another rule that imports other law is Rule 3.4(a), which prohibits lawyers from "unlawfully" obstructing access to evidence. We emphasize the word "unlawfully" because lawyers are free to keep evidence that is harmful to their clients to themselves unless they are under a legal duty to turn it over. Such a duty can arise in numerous ways. A prosecutor has a constitutional obligation to turn over exculpatory evidence to the defense in a criminal case. A lawyer in a civil case must reveal relevant and non-privileged evidence, even if it harms the client, if the other side makes an appropriate discovery request. More generally, lawyers unlawfully conceal evidence when they violate criminal laws regarding obstruction of justice. The federal obstruction of justice statute (18 U.S.C. §1512), for example, makes it a crime for anyone to "corruptly" alter, destroy, mutilate or conceal a record or other object, or attempt to do so, "with the intent to impair the object's integrity or availability for use in an official proceeding."

In a famous example from our part of the world, lawyers sued the DuPont Corporation because its fungicide product, Benlate, allegedly caused harm. The plaintiffs' lawyers sought production of records related to DuPont's testing of Benlate's safety. DuPont produced some but not all of its testing records. When the documents surfaced after the case settled, a federal district judge referred the matter to the U.S. Attorney. DuPont and its lawyers claimed (and still claim) that they engaged in no wrongdoing, and the matter was settled when DuPont agreed to fund four professorial chairs in legal ethics and professionalism at Georgia law schools.

Whether or not DuPont and its lawyers acted unlawfully, the overriding point is this: a lawyer may not unlawfully impede another's access to evidence even if it means that the client will be harmed. The duty of fidelity to the law comes first.

Specific duties relating to fruits, instrumentalities and evidence of client crime

A special application of the lawyer's duty not to unlawfully impede access to evidence arises when lawyers come into possession of the fruits, instrumentalities, or evidence of client crime. For example, a client accused of armed robbery may hand the lawyer the money, the gun, and the written plans used in the crime. The lawyer has a duty to maintain confidentiality but may not "unlawfully" deal with the physical evidence.

The courts have struggled to come up with a coherent and complete set of doctrines that would enable the lawyer to navigate a course between fidelity to the law and fidelity to the client. Although uncertainties remain, some duties are clear. In the most famous example, In Re Ryder, 263 F.Supp. 360 (E.D. Va. 1967), a lawyer took possession of a client's sawed-off shotgun and cash and hid the items in a safe deposit box when the client was charged with using a sawed-off shotgun to rob a bank. The lawyer was suspended from practice for concealing the evidence for the purpose of impeding the client's prosecution. Once the lawyer took possession of the items, the lawyer's obligation was to turn them over to the authorities or at least tell the authorities where they were. In a more recent case, a lawyer for a church destroyed a church laptop that had been used by a church employee and that contained pornographic images of children. The lawyer came to possess the laptop days after the FBI had initiated an investigation of the employee. Although the lawyer claimed not to have knowledge of the investigation—and therefore not to have destroyed the evidence with the intent to impair its availability—he was charged with obstruction of justice and later pleaded guilty to a lesser charge. If this lawyer knew about the investigation, as Ryder knew of the bank robbery, then he could not have destroyed the evidence without violating his duty of fidelity to the law, regardless of the consequences to his client.

The criminal law generally

The old saying is that no one is above the law, and it is certainly true that lawyers are personally bound by the criminal law even while they are representing clients. In the example we just mentioned, the lawyer for the church was charged with the crime of obstruction of justice. Other well-known examples include former Attorney General of the United States John Mitchell and Webster Hubbell, former Associate Attorney General of the United States. Mitchell was found guilty of conspiracy, obstruction of justice, and perjury and sentenced to two and a half to eight years in prison for his role in the Watergate break-in and cover-up. Hubbell was convicted of one count of wire fraud and one count of tax fraud in connection with over-billing at his former law firm and was sentenced to 21 months of imprisonment. Notice that while Hubbell's unlawful behavior occurred in his practice of law, the general criminal law provided the sanction. Lawyers are not above the law, and their duty of fidelity to the law includes the duty not to commit crimes.

WHAT GETS IN THE WAY OF FIDELITY TO THE LAW?

The general duty of fidelity to the law is clear. So why would a lawyer ever violate it? The most common reasons are excess of commitment to a client or cause and the fear of losing and the consequences of losing. Improper conduct can also arise if the lawyer convinces himself that "everyone does it this way" or that "no one will ever know."

Excess commitment to a client or cause

Lawyers are human. They become close to their clients and invested in the success of their client's case. They may truly believe that justice will occur only if the client prevails. Or, they may have such empathy for the client's situation that they overlook the deficiencies of fact or law that will bar the client's success. It is also easy for lawyers to become committed to a cause. For these lawyers, that commitment, which can be positive, may become unchecked and lead to the lawyer's deciding that the cause overrides other considerations. This imbalance can be as harmful to the virtue of fidelity to the law as an excessive commitment to a particular client.

Despite these very human realities, lawyers must temper fidelity to the client (or a cause) with their responsibilities to be faithful to the law. If a lawyer finds himself or herself too committed to the client or the cause, the lawyer will be tempted to cheat. The recent legal troubles of Michael Cohen, former attorney for President Donald Trump, provide an illustration. Cohen blames some of the wrongful acts of which he has been accused, including lying to Congress and tax evasion, on an excess of loyalty to his client, who was his single client for many years. His story, and his incarceration, vividly illustrate the possible consequences of devotion to a client that is allowed to supersede devotion to the law.

Fear

As we have noted before, fear is a powerful motivation, and there are things to be afraid of in the practice of law. If you are in litigation, you will operate in an environment in which opposing counsel is highly trained and highly motivated to see that you fail, to pounce on every misstep. Other professionals do not operate in such a competitive environment. No one plays defense when a surgeon operates. No one is there trying to slap the scalpel away. Because of its adversarial nature, litigation tends to attract competitive people, and competitive people do not like to lose. Maybe you recognize that in yourself. Losing brings consequences—to the ego, to reputation, to the bottom line. Fear of those consequences can lead a lawyer to try to win at any cost. A young prosecutor may fail to turn over exculpatory documents because he fears that doing so would cause him to lose the case, lowering his percentage of successful prosecutions and perhaps jeopardizing a promotion or pay increase. A civil lawyer might "lose" a smoking gun memo during the discovery process because she fears that, if it is revealed, the value of the case is substantially decreased and the firm might lose a client or she might not make partner. Lawyers who lose cases might lose clients.

Fear can also motivate a transactional lawyer. Remember that fidelity to the law requires a lawyer to refuse to help a client commit a crime or a fraud. A transactional lawyer—maybe the lawyers in the OPM debacle—might fear the economic devastation that would follow from saying no to a client who constitutes a large percentage of the firm's business. Saying no will be hard when you feel as if you are punished for doing so.

Never underestimate fear. Whether you eventually engage in litigation or instead do deals for a living, you likely will feel fear that will tempt you to violate your duty of fidelity to the law.

"Everyone does it this way"

One justification given by lawyers for doing such things as destroying evidence, hiding the truth, or making active misrepresentations is that "everyone knows that's the way the game is played." Sometimes instructions to engage in such conduct are prefaced with the (usually patronizing) phrase, "Out here in the real world...." Sometimes the message might be implied rather than overt. If, when they are introduced for the first time to a new client, they are told, "Whatever you do, keep Mr. X happy," they will perceive a message that they are expected to do whatever Mr. X asks, even if it is unlawful. The investigation into Baron & Budd's witness preparation techniques included interviews with young lawyers who revealed that they may have been subject to this kind of pressure when they were instructed to "be creative" when they failed to get helpful information from a client. Subtle pressure may manifest in as simple a way as receiving a negative response from a superior when questioning an action being taken by another lawyer in the office.

Younger lawyers may be particularly susceptible to this rationalization for improper behavior. You will still be learning much about the practice of law, and you will look to those with more experience as a source of learning. You will want to be a "real" lawyer and may be tempted to take at face value what you are taught about how "real lawyers" behave. Do not do that. The professional expectation that you will practice in accordance with the six virtues of the good lawyer is real, no matter that jaded superiors might tell you otherwise.

"No one will ever know"

Finally, you must be aware of the voice in your head that may tell you, when you are tempted to cheat, that "no one will ever know." That voice is not always right. In an era of electronic record-keeping, it is foolhardy to rely on the effective concealment or destruction of a document. But there is an important truth in the statement that no one will ever know. Many of the ways you can cheat are undetectable. A "lawyer's lecture" in the confines of your office is not for public view. A witness instruction to "remember to say you saw the names on the bags" is invisible unless you put it in writing and inadvertently produce it to opposing counsel. Frankly, there are numerous ways to cheat and get away with it. No one will ever know.

But remember that you have excellent reasons to cultivate and deploy the right kind of professional identity even under circumstances where you need not fear any external sanction for not doing so. Part of the punishment for being a cheater is being a cheater. If you rely on the fact that "no one will ever know," you will deny yourself what we described in Chapter 2 as the "internal goods" of the practice of law, the sense of deep satisfaction that comes from conducting yourself in accordance with the best practices of the profession. No one *else* may ever know. But you will.

STRATEGIES FOR CULTIVATING A PROFESSIONAL IDENTITY THAT INCLUDES A DISPOSITION TOWARD FIDELITY TO THE LAW

Develop self-awareness of your motivations

Maintaining awareness of the pressures that may cause you to violate the law in your role of lawyer is crucial. Just as with violation of the other virtues, no lawyer goes into practice intending to violate the civil or criminal law or the rules that govern the practice of law. Yet it happens. Those who succumb to violations of the law because of their roles as attorneys often recount a gradual progression. One small violation leads to another. It becomes easier to hide evidence or mislead the court after having done so once.

You can start right away. Your law school almost certainly has an honor code that sets forth standards for your conduct as a law student. Read it, especially if you have never read it before. Reflect on whether you have observed conduct of your fellow students that may have violated the code. If so, what do you suppose motivated the misconduct? Think about whether you have ever been tempted to do something that would have violated the honor code. If so, what tempted you, and why did you restrain yourself? Was your motivation a fear of getting caught and punished, or was it that you are not the kind of person who cheats? These are just a few mental exercises to begin now to develop a habit of reflection on your motivations and the possible motivations of others.

As an example of how self-awareness can help you once you are a lawyer, imagine that you are dealing with an ambiguous discovery request in a case in which you believe that your client's position is just and that the right result is for your client to prevail. However, you know of a document that, if the other party becomes aware of it, will greatly lessen your chances of success. You have received a poorly drafted discovery request, and it is not clear whether the harmful document is definitely required to be disclosed. If it is, you know that fidelity to the law will require you to turn it over. But you may be able to convince yourself not to produce it—to rationalize such a decision—if you strain to interpret the ambiguous request narrowly and conclude that it has not been requested. As you are making your decision, be aware of the different lenses through which you view the ambiguous request. Do you allow your decision about disclosure to be influenced by how harmful you think the document is to your client's case? Is that a legitimate lens through which to make your decision to disclose? Is your belief in the rightness of your client's case, or perhaps the fear of losing a case for an important client, affecting your interpretation of the discovery request? How can the same words in the same order mean different things depending upon how harmful the document may be to your client? If you find yourself engaging in these mental contortions, your desire to be a zealous advocate may be leading you to violate your obligation to follow the law regarding discovery. Self-awareness is key. Introspection into your motivations is required.

You may face a similar dilemma as a transactional lawyer if you become aware that your client may have misrepresented something to the other side during negotiation. Does the client's action constitute mere puffery, which is permitted under the rules and commonly undertaken? Or, does it go beyond that so that your assistance becomes assistance with a fraud? Is your decision affected by fear of your client's reaction if you challenge the misrepresentation or by an anticipated reaction that others will think you are naïve if you don't go along? The easiest thing would be to decide that your duty of confidentiality means that you do not have to do anything to correct the falsehood and to proceed without having to confront the discomfort of a different action. However, that decision may violate your duty of fidelity to the law. You must ask yourself: why am I doing this?

The overriding lesson, of course, is to be aware of your motivations as you are making decisions of professional judgment and to fully take into your professional identity the virtue of following the law. Self-awareness of your motivations is the starting point of insuring that you will reach a decision consistent with fidelity to the law. Take into account the pressures we have listed above that might lead you astray. Only through a conscious intentionality to manage those pressures in a way that allows you to be faithful to the law will you be able to keep the long-term goals in mind and avoid the short-term pressures that may cause you to do otherwise.

One lawyer has described his own journey to becoming more honest, and therefore less violative of applicable law and standards, in this way:

> *To begin my return to integrity, I decided to notice my lies.*
> *This conscious self-monitoring made me squirm. I hadn't realized how often I succumbed to the temptation to lie—and for how many reasons. I lied to avoid complicated explanations.*

I invented excuses. I rationalized. I manipulated. I failed to disclose. I told outright whoppers. I found that I agreed with another lawyer with whom I discussed lying who said 'It's just easier' than telling the truth....The first step to acting with integrity, therefore is to notice the places where we fail to do so.

(Perlmutter 1998, 126–127)

This lawyer goes on to describe how his self-awareness has resulted in different behavior that is now in sync with his own sense of integrity. He has decided to consistently fulfill the virtue of fidelity to the law.

Practice saying "no" and strive for economic autonomy

Lawyers need to be able to say no to clients when fidelity to the law conflicts with fidelity to the client. A client who wants your help to violate the law—whether it be through the wrongful dismissal of an employee, fraudulently characterizing a transaction to increase the tax benefits, lying on an affidavit, or anything else—can be very insistent. You will naturally approach client interactions and requests with the intent of being helpful. But having developed a habit of self-awareness of your motivations, you will notice when you are tempted to do something improper because the client wants you to. You must be prepared to say no. Practice it. See how it feels to say, "I would like to help you, but I cannot help you violate the law," or "I know that evidence is harmful, but we have to turn it over anyway." Have some stock refusals ready to go in your own mind. You never know when you'll need them.

Saying no becomes even more difficult when the personal economic stakes are high. If the client to whom you must say no is a particularly significant one, your economic self-interest may get in the way of doing the right thing. The stakes are even higher if you are dependent on a single client. As we noted above, fear is a strong motivating force. One way to avoid fear of economic consequences, and avoiding violating the law out of fear of them, is to avoid dependence upon a single client or just a few. It is much easier to say no if one's economic fate is not tied to satisfying one client.

The stakes may also be high if you find yourself in a state of financial distress. Such distress also breeds fear. The more you need the client's fees, the more tempted you may be to earn them even if it means violating your duty of fidelity to the law. Strive for and ferociously defend your financial autonomy. Financial prudence and planning are key to avoid putting yourself in a vulnerable position when your professional responsibility requires that you say no, and a needed client insists that you say yes.

Overall, be sure to look ahead as you are creating the setting in which you will practice law. Diversify your client base. Arrange your financial affairs conservatively. Do what is necessary so that you can turn down a client when you feel that a representation might threaten your ability to act lawfully.

Surround yourself with reminders of your commitment to the law and with people who share it

In some ways, fidelity to the law is less evident in the day-to-day life of a lawyer than some of the other virtues. For example, fidelity to a client is embodied in the person of the client or, if the client is an entity, the client representative with whom you deal. Fidelity to the law is a more abstract concept; its silent demands surround so many different aspects of your life as a lawyer that it may be harder to ensure that the virtue is at the forefront of your mind. Think of ways now to remind yourself of the duty to the law that you soon will undertake. For example, you might keep handy a copy of the law school's honor code, or even just its first page. Similarly, once you are a lawyer you might keep close by a reminder—a framed copy of your attorney's oath, for example—and then it may be more difficult to allow the temptation to serve one client to override your higher duty.

Similarly, surround yourself with others who also take this obligation seriously. Start now with the friends you choose in law school. Once you are in practice, you will find that the challenge described above with workplace ethos is a real one. There are places where the lawyers rely on the maxim that "everyone does it." But the majority of practice settings are ones in which your commitment to the law will be supported and allowed to thrive. When you are seeking out others with whom to work, whether in a firm or law office setting or by association in a particular case, look for those whom you know value being truthful even when it's difficult and who do not articulate some of the justifications for bad behavior we've outlined above. You and they can be mutually reinforcing in the shared commitment to fidelity to the law. Ask each other to help with your commitment. Give permission for someone to challenge you and do the same for them. This intentional building of community around the ethos of fidelity to the law will take you out of the negative culture that the pressures of law may otherwise create. If you find yourself in a work environment that does not provide this support, make a determination to either change the culture or to find another workplace.

CONCLUSION

A lawyer's professional identity must include the virtue of fidelity to the law. It is essential both because of the lawyer's obligation to uphold and advance the law and because this virtue acts as a check on excess commitment to fidelity to the client or a cause. Fidelity to the law includes inherent tensions and complexities, and its origins are diffuse. It arises both from standards that apply only to lawyers and from the general criminal and civil law that binds us all. The complexity of this virtue makes it is especially important that you begin to cultivate habits and dispositions that will support fidelity to the law.

DISCUSSION QUESTIONS AND PROBLEMS

1   Practice implementing your obligation of fidelity to the law in this hypothetical situation (based upon an actual case), paying careful attention to how it might conflict with your duty of fidelity to the client and your desire to be successful in the representation: You are a senior associate in a law firm that is defending a product liability case. Your firm's client is a large pharmaceutical company that is being sued by the parents of a two-year old girl who died after being given a drug for her asthma. The drug was produced by your client under the trade name "Somophylline," the active ingredient of which is known generically as "theophylline." The suit claims that the girl's doctor prescribed Somophylline even though its use was contraindicated because the girl had a viral infection. The suit is against the doctor for medical malpractice and against your client for marketing an unreasonably dangerous product. Crucial issues in the case will be whether in fact the use of Somophylline caused the death of this child and what your client knew about the risks to pediatric patients with viral infections from using Somophylline.

You are responding to discovery requests from the plaintiff, including one that asks that your client to "produce genuine copies of any internal reports or memoranda particularly concerning toxicity of Somophylline Oral Liquid in children." You have found an internal memo from your client's marketing department, dated before the little girl in this case was prescribed Somophylline. The memo reports a "dramatic increase in reports of serious toxicity to theophylline..." and urges that the company should stop promoting theophylline for asthma, and promote Intal instead, because of risks for patients with viral infections.

You know that the requesting party has an obligation to describe "with reasonable particularity" any document it requests and also that your obligation in responding to discovery is to "make reasonably diligent effort to comply with a legally proper discovery request."

Write an essay in which you discuss whether you will produce the internal memo in response to the discovery request. In making your decision and explaining it, pay careful attention to what has influenced you to determine whether you must turn over the document. For example, was your interpretation of what you are required to do influenced by how harmful you think the document is to your client? Should it be? Then research the actual case upon which the hypothetical is based, *Washington State Physicians Insurance Exchange & Association v. Fisons Corporation*, 858 P.2d 1054 (Washington 1993). Does the outcome of the actual case change your mind or your approach to the problem?

2   Think of a time when you have been less than truthful. What motivated you to do so? For example, were you motivated by a desire to avoid hurting someone's feelings? Or, perhaps you were embarrassed by your failure to do something that you should have done and told the lie to avoid revealing your mistake? Or, did you fear the wrath of someone upon learning the truth? Was it just easier, for whatever reason? Write a short reflection in which you describe the incident, your motivations for it, what the consequences were, and what would have had to happen for you to have told the truth instead of lying.

3   Think of a time when you went along with something you didn't want to do because it was the easy thing to do. Perhaps you failed to confront someone when he or she made an inappropriate remark or otherwise acted disrespectfully in a group. Perhaps you agreed to go to a social event even though you didn't want to because you didn't want to hurt someone's feelings. Describe the incident and see if you can identify the reasons that you did not act differently. What steps could you have taken to have handled the situation in another way? Write out a tentative script for the words you could have used to say "no" instead of doing nothing or saying "yes."

4   A prosecutor was sanctioned by a court because he told the court, in response to a question, that he had personally compared the serial numbers on currency seized from the defendant with serial numbers on missing money. In fact, he had not done so, and the serial numbers did not match up. Therefore, the evidence did not prove what was necessary for the prosecutor to win his case: the money that had been in the defendant's possession was not the stolen money. Take a moment to imagine why the prosecutor might have made this misrepresentation to the court. What pressures was he likely experiencing in the moment that the court questioned him that led to the lie? What do you think he was fearful of had he told the truth? How could he have better resolved the various pressures that he was feeling so that he better fulfilled the virtue of fidelity to the law?

5   Arrange an informal interview with a lawyer you know or someone recommended by your law school's faculty or staff. Ask the lawyer whether they have experienced a situation in law

practice in which they were asked to do something inconsistent with the virtue of fidelity to the law. Ask them also whether they have ever witnessed another lawyer acting inconsistently with the virtue of fidelity to the law. Ask them about ways they have handled such situations and any advice they can offer you on how to handle such matters should they arise in your career.

REFERENCE LIST AND SUGGESTED READINGS

Anatomy of a Murder. 1959. Los Angeles: Columbia Pictures.

Biederman, Christine, Thomas Korosec, Julie Lyons, and Patrick Williams. 1998. Toxic Justice. *Dallas Observer.*

Brickman, Lester. 2002. *Asbestos Litigation: Malignancy in the Courts?* www.manhattan-institute.org/html/asbestos-litigation-malignancy-courts-5688.html.

DuBois, Mark A. 2013. Honesty, Integrity and Loyalty. *Essential Qualities of the Professional Lawyer,* ed. Paul A. Haskins. Chicago: ABA Publishing.

Floyd, Daisy Hurst. 1995. Candor vs. Advocacy: Courts' Use of Sanctions to Enforce the Duty of Candor. *Georgia Law Review* 29:1035.

Hodes, W. William. 1999. The Professional Duty to Horseshed Witnesses—Zealously within the Bounds of the Law. *Texas Tech Law Review* 30:1343.

Perlmutter, Mark. 1997. *Why Lawyers Lie and Engage in Other Repugnant Behavior.* Austin: Bright Books.

Rhode, Deborah L. 2000. *In the Interests of Justice: Reforming the Legal Profession.* New York: Oxford University Press.

6

PUBLIC SPIRITEDNESS
AS A PROFESSIONAL VIRTUE

INTRODUCTION

We hear in every bar association luncheon or "welcome to law school" speech that the legal profession is a service profession, and that at its core it is about public service. You probably sat through one of these speeches during your orientation. Those statements are no less true for having been repeated in trite ways thousands of times. Many years ago, Roscoe Pound famously defined a "profession" as

> *a group ... pursuing a learned art as a common calling in the spirit of public service—no less a public service because it may incidentally be a means of livelihood. Pursuit of the learned art in the spirit of a public service is the primary purpose.*
>
> *(Pound 1944, 203)*

He was exactly right in one respect: public service is central to what it means to be a professional lawyer.

Even in his own day, however, Pound was wrong about the practice of law being "incidentally" a means of livelihood. Lawyers are entitled to make a living, and most are well compensated for their work, usually by their clients. Lawyers have always felt some tension between serving the public and making a living. As we will see, one reason why lawyers do not do more to serve the public interest is the cost to themselves in time and money.

Nonetheless, as a lawyer you will have a privileged position in society, and in return for that position you will be justifiably expected to practice in the spirit of public service. Having a disposition toward serving the public good is an essential virtue for lawyers. In this chapter we will explore in concrete terms what it means to practice in a spirit of public service, we will discuss factors that may prevent many lawyers from serving the public interest, and we will suggest strategies for cultivating a disposition to public spiritedness in your work.

WHAT DOES "PRACTICING IN A SPIRIT OF PUBLIC SERVICE" MEAN FOR LAWYERS?

It is one thing to make broad pronouncements that lawyers should practice in a spirit of public service. It is another to put that commitment into concrete action. In a democracy, all citizens—not just lawyers—should have some concern for the public welfare and participate in governance. For you as a lawyer, however, your status as an officer of the court and a guardian of our justice system will place particular responsibilities on you. Practicing in a spirit of public service for the legal profession means at least the following:

- *working to ensure access to justice for all persons, including representing those who cannot afford a lawyer and representing unpopular causes and clients;*
- *regulating the profession in order to serve the public interest; and*
- *working to improve the law and legal institutions.*

Ensuring access to justice: equal justice under law

"Equal Justice Under Law" are the words engraved on the front of the United States Supreme Court building. In many ways, this is the high temple of the American legal system, and those words are the most important summary of our legal principles. Indeed, children for generations have begun the school day by reciting the Pledge of Allegiance, closing with the words "with liberty and justice for all."

The theory of justice in American society is based fundamentally upon equality before the law. This means that every person, without regard to race, sex, national origin, religion, or other category, has the same rights under the law and an equal opportunity to assert those rights. Moreover, a person's wealth or poverty should make no difference to a court. The iconic statue of Lady Justice wears the blindfold to symbolize the equality of rich and poor before the law. These principles are derived in part from the Biblical injunctions "to judge impartially, and do not favor the wealthy," and that the law should be "no respecter of persons."

The United States has an adversary legal system; one feature of that system is that it places the burden on the parties to bring, investigate, prepare, and present their own cases. The complexity of the legal system necessitates the representation of parties by competent persons who have been trained to navigate it. Any party without a lawyer is at a serious disadvantage in presenting a case with a chance of success. If parties frequently must appear without the benefit of a lawyer, the system is simply not living up to the promise of equal justice under law. In the words of Justice Nathan Hecht of the Texas Supreme Court, "if we don't have justice for all, we don't have justice at all" (Daedalus 2019, 190).

Access to justice and the justice gap

Unfortunately, a significant number of persons are forced to navigate the justice system without counsel, solely because they do not have the means to hire a lawyer. In criminal cases, ever since *Gideon v. Wainwright*, 372 U.S. 335 (1963), legal assistance for those who cannot afford a lawyer has been a constitutional right. States have not always complied with the mandate of *Gideon* to provide adequate funding for indigent legal services, and public defenders and appointed counsel often struggle with overwhelming caseloads, making it difficult to provide competent and effective representation to each individual client. But, however limited the assistance may be in some jurisdictions, all persons accused of crime are entitled to a lawyer.

However, there is no corresponding right to counsel in civil matters. Most low-income Americans, and many middle-income Americans, are forced to go it alone without legal representation. This has led to what has been termed "the justice gap." The most recent and thorough study of the legal needs of low-income American is the 2017 Report of the Legal Services Corporation (LSC), entitled *The Justice Gap: Measuring the Unmet Civil Legal Needs of Low-income Americans*. This Report found:

- *In 2016, 86% of the civil legal problems reported by low-income Americans received inadequate or no legal help.*
- *71% of low-income households experienced at least one civil legal problem in the previous year, including problems with health care, housing conditions, disability access, veterans' benefits, and domestic violence.*
- *Low-income Americans approached LSC-funded legal aid organizations for support with an estimated 1.7 million problems. They received only limited or no legal help for more than half of these problems due to a lack of resources for the legal services offices.*

In 2016, of the 71% of low-income households that experienced at least one civil legal problem during the year, only 14% received legal help in dealing with the problems they reported (Legal Services Corporation 2017, 13–14). Moreover, "people often do not realize that their problem has a legal dimension. Human miseries that could be alleviated continue and cascade into disasters, jeopardizing the legitimacy of the legal system itself" (Daedalus 2019, 8).

Civil cases do not pose the same risks of harm as criminal cases, in which the state may send the defendant to prison or in extreme cases take the defendant's life. But when a landlord locks somebody out of his or her home, or when a creditor takes someone's life savings, or when a government agency terminates someone's food stamps or SSI check, or when a child welfare agency takes away a child, the consequences are nonetheless enormous.

Another measure of the justice gap is the rapidly growing number of unrepresented litigants who proceed in court on their own, or "pro se." In almost three quarters of domestic cases in state courts, one or both parties go unrepresented. Pro se litigants are far more likely to fail, especially when they are opposed by a party who is represented by a lawyer. In some subject matter areas, this imbalance is common: in housing court, more than 90% of tenants facing eviction have no lawyer, while more than 90% of the landlords do (Daedalus 2019, 8).

People lack access to justice because the law is complex; therefore, it is usually essential to have a lawyer to guide, counsel, and advocate for any party with something at stake in the system. But in part because the law is complex, it can also be expensive to hire a lawyer. For that reason, the justice gap is not just a reality for poor people, that is, those who cannot afford to pay anything. Many persons with moderate incomes who could afford modest legal fees are effectively priced out of the market. Many of those people end up unrepresented if they are in litigation, or they forego possible legal remedies for their problems.

The responsibility to perform pro bono service

One answer to the problem posed by the justice gap is for lawyers to represent low income persons for no fee (known as *pro bono publico* representation, "for the public good") or for a substantially reduced fee (sometimes referred to as "low bono" representation). In fact, the Model Rules of Professional Conduct assert that lawyers have a responsibility to render pro bono service to persons who cannot afford a lawyer. Rule 6.1, entitled "Voluntary Pro Bono Publico Service," states: "Every lawyer has a professional responsibility to provide legal services to those unable to pay. A lawyer should aspire to render at least (50) hours of pro bono publico legal services per year…." The Rule goes on to state that lawyers should

> *provide a substantial majority of the (50) hours of legal services without fee or expectation of fee to: (1) persons of limited means or (2) charitable, religious, civic, community, governmental and educational organizations in matters that are designed primarily to address the needs of persons of limited means.*

Notably, although the rule speaks of the "professional responsibility" to do pro bono work, it does not actually require lawyers to provide any pro bono representation. Notice the words "should aspire to render" rather than any mandatory language. In other words, lawyers are not subject to disciplinary sanction if they fail to do pro bono work. It is an aspiration rather than a mandate. Several jurisdictions and bar associations have explored whether pro bono service should be mandatory for some or all lawyers. Courts and commissions from New York to Mississippi to California have recommended some form of mandatory pro bono. By and large, those efforts have been rejected. Indeed, the original early draft of what became Rule 6.1 of the Model Rules would have required lawyers to perform 40 hours of pro bono service or its equivalent per year, but the final version of the Rule rejected any mandatory duty, including even a requirement that lawyers report their pro bono hours. Currently no state imposes a pro bono requirement, although some states do require that lawyers report annually their hours devoted to pro bono service. Several more states invite voluntary reporting of pro bono hours.

Pressures to make pro bono service mandatory continue. Beginning in 2015, all applicants for admission to the bar in the state of New York are required to perform a minimum of 50 hours of qualified pro bono service as a condition for admission to the bar. To date, no other state has followed suit in requiring pre-admission pro bono of bar applicants. But because the unmet need for legal services for the poor in civil matters is so great, we can expect calls for mandatory pro bono to continue. Indeed, in a speech in 2016 on access to justice issues, Justice Sonia Sotomayor stated, "if I had my way, I would make pro bono service a requirement" (Mauro 2016).

A recent study by the American Bar Association sheds light on how many lawyers actually do pro bono work. The study surveyed more than 50,000 attorneys in 24 states, seeking data in such areas as their interest, time spent, and key influencing factors related to pro bono work. Although over 80% of attorneys said that they believed pro bono work is very important, only about half had performed any pro bono work in the previous year. Less than 20% provided the aspirational amount of 50 hours during the previous year. About 20% reported that they had never done any pro bono work. The reason most lawyers gave for not doing more pro bono work was a lack of time (American Bar Association 2018).

Other ways of closing the justice gap

More pro bono by lawyers would help to close the justice gap, but even if all lawyers performed the aspirational goal of 50 pro bono hours per year, lawyers still would not meet all the legal needs of the poor and the middle class. Over the past couple of decades, other strategies to address the justice gap by making legal services more accessible and affordable have developed.

One such strategy is the legal incubator movement. Legal incubators provide mentoring and support to new lawyers interested in launching their own solo practices. Though their missions vary, the majority of incubators focus on the delivery of legal services to under-represented populations, and they emphasize new ways to serve clients in less expensive ways, including use of innovative technology. The first legal incubator was created in 2007, and there are now more than 70 incubators in the United States (American Bar Association 2019).

Another option to making legal services more accessible and affordable is to allow certain legal services to be rendered by non-lawyers. State laws generally prohibit the practice of law without a law license; this is the unauthorized practice of law, also known as "UPL." It is routine, however, for paralegals to serve clients, but they generally may do so only under the direct supervision of a lawyer. The State of Washington has created a process for the licensure of Limited License Legal Technicians (LLLTs), non-lawyers who can provide certain legal services independently, without such supervision (State of Washington 2019). The premise is that, by freeing "legal technicians" from the necessity of being supervised by attorneys, the LLLTs can serve certain clients' legal needs at a lower cost than lawyers can. A rough analogy might be the increasing reliance on nurse practitioners and physicians' assistants in the medical field. Other states are considering similar proposals to license paraprofessionals to serve clients in certain areas. To date, however, very few persons have been licensed as legal technicians.

The private market has also responded with efforts to make legal services more accessible and affordable. Websites that provide online legal help to people, such as LegalZoom and Rocket Lawyer, have proliferated. And there are mobile apps that provide legal tips and information about a wide range of legal problems, all the way from parking tickets to traffic stops to immigration issues. Online resources as well as legal assistance by paraprofessionals may help with the justice gap but also raise issues regarding the need for restrictions on the UPL.

The legal profession has fought many innovations in the delivery of legal services on the premise that the public needs to be protected from unauthorized, and therefore incompetent, legal assistance. We will discuss later in this chapter how the profession must be careful to approach such regulation only with the interests of the public in mind.

Representation of unpopular causes and clients

Closely related to the duty to represent those who cannot pay for legal services is the duty to represent unpopular causes and clients. The principle of Equal Justice under Law requires that that all persons, no matter how unpopular, are entitled to equal access to the courts, and to representation when they are accused of a crime. Model Rule of Professional Conduct 6.2 requires that lawyers accept appointments by the court unless there is good cause not to do so. The rule allows lawyers to seek to avoid an appointment only in limited circumstances: when the representation would violate the ethical rules (e.g., it would create an impermissible conflict of interest); when the representation would impose severe financial hardship on the attorney; and when the lawyer finds the client or the cause so repugnant that the lawyer cannot provide effective representation. The rule embodies the idea that lawyers are expected to do their fair share of representing unpopular causes and clients. Because there is a constitutional right to counsel in criminal but not civil cases, appointments are far more likely in criminal cases. Nonetheless, in many jurisdictions judges appoint lawyers to represent children in custody cases, parents in termination cases, and other areas in which the need for counsel is especially great. Courts generally appoint lawyers who have volunteered for appointments and who have some experience in the area of law, and there is usually provision for modest payment to appointed lawyers.

The profession celebrates lawyers fictional (Atticus Finch) and real (Clarence Darrow) who undertake such work. Most of this work, however, is done as a routine matter every day by public defenders, usually at salaries that are much lower than average for lawyers. Almost by definition, someone accused of a crime, certainly any violent crime, is an unpopular client; criminal defense lawyers often face the question "how can you defend someone like that?" Yet defense lawyers day in and day out represent such people and justifiably see it as a public service.

Self-regulation of the profession

The legal profession must be independent of external regulation if it is to fulfill its public purposes, including especially the protection of unpopular clients. Key to that independence is the profession's right to regulate itself. But you must always remember that society grants the profession the privilege of self-regulation in order to *protect the public*. Lawyers are entrusted with the responsibility to protect and improve our justice system; an essential aspect of that is ensuring that lawyers are competent and ethical. Sometimes lawyers, individually and collectively, forget that all regulation of the profession must benefit the public. A bar association is *not* a guild or a trade association whose purpose is to protect and enrich its own members. The purpose of the organized bar is to be to regulate the profession in ways that protect the public and clients.

Self-regulation includes both the regulation and discipline of attorneys who are already licensed and the admission of new attorneys to the profession. In the vast majority of the states, both discipline and bar admission are within the jurisdiction of the state's highest court. As the head of the judicial branch, state supreme courts possess the authority to regulate the profession, under the state constitution, statutory law, or the court's inherent power. Courts in many states rely heavily upon volunteer lawyers to do much of the day-to-day work in both bar admission and bar discipline.

Although many lawyers do serve roles in the lawyer disciplinary system, most lawyers are not directly involved in its operation. Nonetheless, all lawyers have a responsibility for the discipline of lawyers. Model Rule 8.3(a) requires a lawyer to report another lawyer's misconduct to disciplinary authorities:

> *(a) A lawyer who knows that another lawyer has committed a violation of the Rules of Professional Conduct that raises a substantial question as to that lawyer's honesty, trustworthiness or fitness as a lawyer in other respects, shall inform the appropriate professional authority.*

Note that the rule does not require lawyers to report *all* suspected misconduct by another lawyer. The requirement only applies to violations that the lawyer actually knows occurred (as opposed to those the lawyer suspects or believes has occurred), and the duty to report only applies to violations that raise serious questions about the lawyer's trustworthiness or general fitness to practice law. It is subject to the lawyer's duty of confidentiality to the client. Nonetheless, subject to those limitations, the duty is real, and a lawyer who fails to report professional misconduct as covered by Rule 8.3(a) may be subject to discipline, including potentially the ultimate sanction of disbarment.

Moreover, all lawyers have a responsibility to cooperate with lawyer disciplinary authorities. It is a violation to make a false statement or to fail to disclose information necessary to correct a misapprehension in connection with such matters. And Rule 8.1 requires lawyers to respond to requests for information from disciplinary bodies.

The lawyer's responsibility for the regulation of the profession extends to the process of admission to the bar. The same basic requirements as to disciplinary cases apply to lawyer admissions matters. Lawyers must be truthful and responsive in any matter involving the admissions process for applicants to the bar. Every jurisdiction requires that applicants to the bar are subject to some form of a "character and fitness" inquiry. The examining authorities are tasked with making sure that prospective lawyers are not likely to engage in conduct that could harm their future clients.

We noted above in the discussion of "legal technicians" and legal help websites that all states prohibit UPL. The purpose of regulating UPL is to protect the public from persons who are not trained in the law and not capable of providing competent assistance. Although unauthorized practice restrictions are designed to protect the public, it is easy for such restrictions to operate in ways that protect the self-interest of lawyers who do not want a cheaper alternative to their services to be available. For example, a number of years ago Texas lawyers successfully opposed the sale of a CD-ROM product called "Quicken Lawyer" that guided purchasers to create legal documents much as TurboTax now does for tax returns. The Texas legislature quickly overruled the lawyers and allowed consumers to purchase Quicken Lawyer.

Self-interested application of unauthorized practice restrictions has the potential to undercut access to justice. For persons who cannot afford to pay, those who cannot afford to pay market rates, and those who might find it difficult to find a lawyer, easing the restrictions on UPL may help to provide needed legal help. But it is crucial that any provision of legal help by non-lawyers be effective and competent. For the profession as a whole, the key is to recognize that self-regulation, including the restrictions on unauthorized practice, exists for the sole purpose of protecting the public.

Improvement of the law

The Preamble to the Model Rules states:

> As a public citizen, a lawyer should seek improvement of the law …. As a member of a learned profession, a lawyer should cultivate knowledge of the law beyond its use for clients, employ that knowledge in reform of the law and work to strengthen legal education. In addition, a lawyer should further the public's understanding of and confidence in the rule of law and the justice system because legal institutions in a constitutional democracy depend on popular participation and support to maintain their authority.

You will likely find many opportunities to engage in public service apart from representation of clients. Lawyers are regularly asked to serve on the board of directors of nonprofit organizations. Serving on the board of indigent legal services organizations can help to ensure that the mission of equal justice for all is served. There are many other nonprofit organizations that work to improve the law in areas such as civil rights, election law, environmental law, and countless other areas. If there is an area of public policy that you care deeply about, there are almost certainly organizations working in that area. Volunteering in their work and serving on boards and committees of such organizations is a valuable service.

Lawyers are often asked to serve on commissions and boards at the local and state level. Many positive reforms in the law, such as restorative justice initiatives in criminal justice, more collaborative processes in family law, protection of children in the foster care system, and many more such efforts, have been the product of study commissions appointed to suggest changes to existing law. Lawyers play an essential role in these law reform efforts. It can be enormously rewarding to work toward positive systemic changes in an area that you care about.

Lawyers play an even more direct role in law-making by serving in legislative bodies at the local, state, and national level. Lawyers can provide an important voice in legislatures. For example, lawyer-legislators are more likely to support independence of the judiciary and funding for civil legal aid. However, the number of lawyers who serve in legislative bodies has been declining. The percentage of lawyers serving in state legislatures dropped from 22.3% in 1976 to 14.4% in 2015 (Fifield 2015). And although a higher percentage of members of the United States Congress are lawyers, there has been a slow, but steady, decline in their numbers. In the mid-nineteenth century, almost 80% of members of Congress were lawyers. By the 1960s, this dropped to under 60%, and in 2017, the number of lawyer-members in Congress was slightly under 40% (Robinson 2017, 659). The rule of law and the principle of equal justice may depend upon more lawyers being willing to serve as legislators.

WHAT CAUSES LAWYERS NOT TO PRACTICE IN A SPIRIT OF PUBLIC SERVICE?

The professional duty to practice in a spirit of public service is clear. As with the other virtues, however, there are obstacles to the cultivation and deployment of the virtue of public-spiritedness. These obstacles include time demands, the temptation to protect ourselves, and other barriers.

Time demands

The primary reason why lawyers fail to serve the public interest is time. Lawyers are busy people. Many lawyers are stretched pretty thin, from increasing demands from their employers, to the increasing connectivity that means that one is never truly "away" from work, to the demands of raising and caring for family members. Even when lawyers would like to provide pro bono representation and perform other public service activities, it can be difficult to justify the time commitment, especially uncompensated time.

The Pro Bono Survey revealed that lack of time is the principal reason why lawyers do not do more pro bono work (American Bar Association 2018). It is true that pro bono work in particular can be time consuming. Often the greatest need for legal services is in relatively specialized legal areas that many lawyers are unfamiliar with, such as family law, consumer issues, and access to government benefits. Taking on cases in these areas may take more time than representing a client in a matter in which the lawyer regularly practices. Some lawyers also worry, perhaps with some justification, that clients who need help in personal plight cases such as family law or bankruptcy will demand an inordinate amount of the lawyer's time to discuss the issues.

On the other hand, it may be that lawyers' fears of the time needed for pro bono are exaggerated. Lawyers may properly limit the scope of representation so that they need not be drawn into a myriad of unrelated problems. Moreover, legal services offices, which are the referral source for much pro bono work, provide many resources such as forms and training to ease the time demands associated with taking on a case.

Succumbing to the temptation to protect ourselves

Another barrier to public spiritedness arises in the area of self-regulation. As you will see in more detail in Chapter 9, you are entering the profession at a time of economic disruption generally, and the legal profession is not immune to disruption. With disruption come fear and the instinct to protect ourselves. The profession comes to see developments that improve access to legal services, that make court procedures simpler, or that otherwise reduce the demand for our services as threats to our livelihoods rather than as opportunities to benefit the public. It can be too easy in such circumstances to forget that society allows the legal profession to regulate itself on the condition that we will do so solely in order to serve the public interest. Lawyers sometimes speak of the profession's "right" to regulate itself. Self-regulation is not something to which the profession is entitled; self-regulation is a privilege. That privilege is abused when the profession protects its own interests in the drafting of the rules of conduct or in the handing of disciplinary matters. The temptation to protect the guild and its members is real and understandable, but giving in to that temptation is one reason why lawyers sometimes do not practice in the spirit of public service.

Other barriers

Some well-meaning lawyers express discomfort at taking on pro bono clients for fear that they will not know how to handle the kinds of matters that poor people need handled. These lawyers believe in serving the poor but fear doing more harm than good. Going through a pro bono referral agency is a good way to select cases in which the lawyer feels comfortable. There are many relatively simple matters that any lawyer can handle. And as noted, these agencies provide much support to lawyers who agree to take on a case.

Other lawyers may believe on principle that providing legal services to the poor is a societal problem and should be resolved by the broader society, perhaps by public financial support of legal services, rather than by the legal profession alone. Those are valid sentiments. Society does have an obligation to ensure access to justice for all. But as we have shown, lawyers have a special responsibility for the quality of justice. Providing direct pro bono service is a part of that responsibility. In addition, the reality is that society does not fund existing legal services programs at anything close to a level that can meet unmet legal needs. To decline to help under such circumstances is like being the only person who can swim and declining to assist a drowning man because the county should have paid for a lifeguard. Unless and until legal services agencies can meet that need, lawyers must do their part.

Failure to do voluntary pro bono is sometimes expressed as function of resentment of the cost of legal education and the accompanying skyrocketing debt loads of many law graduates. You might be thinking (and we have heard students say): "If I am going to pay all this money, and pay back all these loans, then I'll be damned if I am going to work for free." We understand. Legal education is expensive. But that is not the fault of the poor who need a little help that only we can provide. We hope that in time you will come to believe that law school was worth every penny, and that the opportunity to spend one's life doing meaningful work—sometimes even for free—is not a cause of resentment but rather should be a cause for gratitude. But if you do not reach that conclusion, we nevertheless urge you to work directly to lower the cost of legal education rather than inflict collateral damage by refusing to help people who need you.

Other young lawyers may calculate the "cost" of a pro bono hour by seeing the work as something that does not count toward fulfillment of a billable hour quota imposed by an employer. Most young lawyers work for law firms or other organizations. Providing pro bono representation in these circumstances is not a direct financial cost to the employed lawyer. But some employers support and encourage pro bono work and some do not. Giving proper credit and support for such work goes a long way in overcoming reluctance by new lawyers. You should seek to discern ahead of time whether prospective employers will provide support and encouragement.

STRATEGIES FOR CULTIVATING A PROFESSIONAL IDENTITY THAT INCLUDES A DISPOSITION TO PUBLIC SERVICE

The legal profession exists to serve the public interest in the ways we have described. If lawyers are to fulfill their public purposes, their collective efforts must be conducted in a spirit of public spiritedness.

As an individual lawyer, however, you should not feel daunted by this responsibility. Practicing law is still a means of earning a living, and there will be ample opportunity to be financially successful. No one is expected to devote most of their time to non-compensated public service; and no one individual can spend time in each of the areas of public service that we have described above.

But public service, in whatever way bests suits your own interests and abilities, is something you should explore, for your own well-being. True satisfaction in life always involves some degree of service to others and to the common good. Self-Determination Theory teaches us that you have a fundamental psychological need for relatedness and that your sense of well-being is much more tied to activities you engage in for their intrinsic value rather than for extrinsic rewards such as money. Our pitch to you is that you will find relatedness and intrinsic rewards when you serve others who need you, maybe even especially when they cannot afford to pay you. Recall also Frederick Buechner's definition of vocation or calling, as "the place where your deep gladness and the world's deep hunger meet." If you cultivate a disposition to public service, and seek out opportunities to serve in areas that you care deeply about, you will find that public service can be a richly rewarding part of your life and your work. Here are a few suggestions on how to start.

Represent a client pro bono even if you are reluctant to do so

We have found from talking to countless law students and new lawyers over the years that lawyers who undertake pro bono representation, even reluctantly, find that it is an enriching and meaningful experience. For those who were reluctant, they often found to their surprise that they came back and volunteered to do more. Volunteering to do pro bono work as a law student (under supervision of a lawyer, of course) or as a new lawyer can be an excellent way to hone skills and learn about new areas of the law. Most who do represent an indigent client in a civil matter also discover the satisfaction of making a difference in someone's life.

Interview a public defender, prosecutor, or legal services lawyer about his or her work

Many of the most fulfilled and satisfied lawyers we know are public defenders, prosecutors, and lawyers for civil legal services offices. Although they make salaries that tend to be well below those of their peers in the profession, many express deep satisfaction in their work. The satisfaction comes from knowing that they are serving the public good and making a difference for the better in people's lives. You don't need to take our word for it; you can hear directly about the rewards and challenges of this type of work by seeking out and interviewing these lawyers.

We noted above that many members of the public don't understand how an attorney can represent people accused of crimes. To get a better idea about what it's like to represent "those people," meet with someone who does that work on a regular basis. You may get an intriguing answer about the pride in standing up to the power of the state on behalf of someone who has no one else to stand with him, or the satisfaction in defending the constitution. A prosecutor may tell you about the satisfaction in serving as a minister of justice rather than someone whose focus is mainly on winning. A legal services lawyer will no doubt have many stories of clients who were able to stay in their homes, or obtained a protective order against an abuser, or maintained custody of children, thanks to the lawyer's representation.

Read about lawyers who have served the public

There is no shortage of inspiring stories about lawyers who have made a profound impact on the justice system and in the lives of their clients. One of the best examples is Bryan Stevenson, the founder of Equal Justice Initiative in Alabama. His memoir, Just Mercy, tells of his representation of death row inmates and others accused of serious crimes (Stevenson 2014). Stevenson dealt with hostility and even threats of violence for his representation of persons whom society found to be repugnant, but he eloquently describes the humanity of his clients and the close relationships he formed with them. In addition to their inspiring work on behalf of persons facing the death penalty, Stevenson and his colleagues at EJI have dramatically changed the law in the United States with regard to the sentencing of juveniles.

There are numerous other examples. Praying for Sheetrock by Melissa Faye Green is an inspiring (and beautifully written) book about a team of legal services lawyers in one rural Georgia County (Green 1991). The lawyers helped to empower a local community to overcome centuries of oppression, profoundly changing the social dynamics of the county. Uncommon Sense: The Achievement of Griffin Bell tells the story of Griffin Bell, who served as Attorney General in the Carter administration (Murphy 2001). After the crimes and betrayal of public trust of the Watergate scandal, Bell brought integrity and independence to the Justice Department. And so on. If you find such reading inspires you, ask your mentors and professors for more suggestions. One of the lawyers we have involved regularly in our course on professional identity makes it a practice to distribute to our students a reading list of "must reads for law students." The list is now several single-spaced pages long. Start making your own list.

Become involved in your local or state bar association

Self-regulation and the legal profession's efforts to improve the law occur most often through bar associations. Many have law student or young lawyer divisions with which you can become involved. In our experience, lawyers who become involved in bar associations often manifest the virtue of public spiritedness—and most are eager to welcome law students and new lawyers to their midst. Of course, joining a bar association is also a great way to meet practicing lawyers and to build your network. But you can also observe directly lawyers who volunteer their time to improve the profession and the legal system, and thereby see for yourself what it means to act with public spiritedness. You can become part of the long and grand tradition of lawyers selflessly serving the public.

CONCLUSION

A lawyer's professional identity must include an internalized personal commitment to the public interest. As we have seen, public spiritedness for lawyers is more than a general sense of caring about the public good. As a lawyer, you will have a responsibility to ensure access to justice for all, to regulate the profession for the benefit of the public, and to work to improve the law and the legal system. You can cultivate a disposition to serve in these ways, and in so doing, you may find that you find your own calling in the law.

DISCUSSION QUESTIONS AND PROBLEMS

1 Should the provision of pro bono service each year be a requirement for every lawyer, as a condition of continued licensure? If so, how much service should be required? How would you define qualifying service? If pro bono service should not be required, why not?

2 Should some form of pro bono service after starting law school be required as a condition of admission to the bar? If so, how much service should be required? How would you define qualifying service? If pro bono service should not be required, why not?

3 Review the requirements for becoming a LLLT in Washington. Discuss whether such an opportunity, or something similar, should be available in your state. What is the benefit to the public of allowing LLLTs to practice? Is there any downside to the public in allowing such practitioners? What is the likely impact on the legal profession of allowing legal technicians to practice as per the Washington regulations?

4 Part of the responsibility of self-regulation is ensuring that persons who seek admission to practice will be worthy of the trust and confidence that future clients will place in them. What negative factors do you think are most essential for "Character and Fitness" Boards to consider in bar applicants? Criminal records? Arrests that did not lead to conviction? Financial irresponsibility? History of alcohol or other substance abuse? Academic dishonesty such as plagiarism? Other factors? Why do any of these factors matter in considering the admission of new attorneys?

5 Another aspect of the responsibility of self-regulation is reporting misconduct by other lawyers. Imagine that you are litigating a case against a lawyer who is constantly late for meetings and often ignores your emails and other requests for information. You suspect that he is having personal problems, often appearing unkempt and showing up for depositions with alcohol

on his breath. You also are convinced that he has not done necessary legal research and factual investigation on behalf of his client. How serious does his incompetence have to be for you to consider reporting him to bar disciplinary authorities? What other factors would you consider in deciding whether to report the misconduct?

6   Complete the following sentence. "I know it is part of my responsibility to represent unpopular causes and clients. I COULD represent a client who _____. I COULD NOT represent a client who _____." Be ready to explain your responses, both to an audience of lawyers and to a friend or family member who is not a lawyer.

REFERENCE LIST AND SUGGESTED READINGS

American Bar Association. 2018. *Supporting Justice: A Report on the Pro Bono Work of America's Lawyers* (extensive survey of American lawyers regarding pro bono work—full report available at www.americanbar. org/content/dam/aba/administrative/probono_public_service/ls_pb_supporting_justice_iv_final.pdf).

American Bar Association Resource and Directory of Lawyer Incubators. 2019. www.americanbar. org/groups/delivery_legal_services/initiatives_awards/program_main/.

Brown, Lonnie T. Jr. 2007. Representing Saddam Hussein. *Georgia Law Review* 42:47.

Cramton, Roger C. 1994. Delivery of Legal Services to Ordinary Americans. *Case Western Reserve Law Review* 44:531.

Daedalus: The Journal of the American Academy of Arts and Sciences. 2019. www.amacad.org/daedalus/access-to-justice.

Fagelson, David. 1999. Rights and Duties: The Ethical Obligation to Serve the Poor. *Law and Inequality: A Journal of Theory and Practice* 17:171.

Fifield, Joan. 2015. State Legislatures Have Fewer Farmers, Lawyers. *Pew Trust The Demographics of State Legislatures.* www.pewtrusts.org/en/research-and-analysis/blogs/stateline/2015/12/10/state-legislatures-have-fewer-farmers-lawyers-but-higher-education-level.

Green, Melissa Fay. 1991. *Praying for Sheetrock.* Cambridge: De Capo Press.

Legal Services Corporation. 2017. *The Justice Gap: Measuring the Unmet Civil Legal Needs of Low-income Americans.* www.lsc.gov/media-center/publications/2017-justice-gap-report.

Mauro, Tony. 2016. Sotomayor Urges Pro Bono for All Lawyers. *National Law Journal.* www.law. comalmlD/1202757812765/pro-bono/.

Murphy, Reg. 2001. *Uncommon Sense: The Achievement of Griffin Bell.* Atlanta: Longstreet Press.

The National Center for Access to Justice. 2016. *The Justice Index* (online resource of findings, indicators, indexing and other data-analytics tools to help ensure that a person's ability to protect and vindicate her rights in a state justice system does not depend on whether she can afford a lawyer). https://justiceindex.org/.

New York Court of Appeals. 2019. *Rules of the Court of Appeals for the Admission of Attorneys and Counselors at Law.* www.nycourts.gov/ctapps/520rules10.htm#B16.

Pound, Roscoe. 1944. What is a Profession – the Rise of the Legal Profession in Antiquity. *Notre Dame Law Review* 19:201.

Robinson, Nick. 2017. The Decline of the Lawyer Politician. *Buffalo Law Review* 65:657.

State of Washington Rules and Regulations for Limited License Legal Technicians. 2019. www.wsba. org/for-legal-professionals/join-the-legal-profession-in-wa/limited-license-legal-technicians.

Stevenson, Bryan. 2014. *Just Mercy.* New York: Speigel and Grau.

7

CIVILITY AS A PROFESSIONAL VIRTUE

INTRODUCTION

We saw in Chapter 1 that civility is one of the six virtues of the professional lawyer that are necessary for lawyers to fulfill their public purposes. Unlike competence, fidelity to the client, and fidelity to the law, civility is not directly regulated by any of the Model Rules of Professional Conduct, although there are a few references to it scattered around the rules. The Preamble mentions "the lawyer's obligation zealously to protect and pursue a client's legitimate interests ... while maintaining a professional, courteous and civil attitude toward all persons involved in the legal system." Comment 3 to Rule 1.3, concerning diligence, provides in part: "A lawyer's duty to act with reasonable promptness, however, does not preclude the lawyer from agreeing to a reasonable request for a postponement that will not prejudice the lawyer's client." Model Rule 8.5(e) provides that it is misconduct to engage in conduct that is prejudicial to the administration of justice. A few states have in recent years begun to treat civility as a disciplinary matter, and some courts have dealt with it under their inherent power, but in the 1980s, when the modern professionalism movement began, there was nothing, or next to nothing, that directly prohibited incivility.

The 1980s, a time of enormous growth in the legal profession, saw an explosion of reports of uncivil conduct among lawyers. As a result, no subject has been more closely associated with the modern professionalism movement in the United States than civility. Every one of the more than 140 codes, creeds and other aspirational statements that courts and bar associations have promulgated about lawyer professionalism contains some language about the need for lawyers to display civility. Still, reports of uncivil conduct by lawyers appear frequently in the legal and popular press, and indeed some lawyers take great pride in advertising themselves as "pit bulls" or "hammers." A 2014 survey of Illinois lawyers found that 85% of those surveyed had experienced some form of incivility or other unprofessional behavior within the last six months (National Center for Professional and Research Ethics 2014). That finding corresponded closely to the findings of other lawyer surveys in earlier years.

In this chapter, we will examine the virtue of civility. We will start by exploring what the profession means by "civility" so that you will be sensitized to recognize it, and recognize its opposite, incivility. We will examine what causes lawyers to engage in uncivil conduct, in order to sensitize you to the circumstances in which challenges to your civility could arise. We then take a look at some strategies for dealing with another's incivility and your own temptation to be uncivil in order to provide some guidance as you attempt to implement a decision to conduct yourself with civility.

WHAT DOES "CIVILITY" MEAN FOR LAWYERS?

Bar associations and courts have used various definitions of what they mean by "civility." One set of recommendations regarding civility, from the Committee on Civility of the Seventh Judicial Circuit, has been more influential than others (Committee on Civility of the Seventh Federal Judicial Circuit 1992). The Seventh Circuit Standards were proposed after an extensive survey of lawyers in the circuit. We will use them as an example of a thoughtful and representative statement from the bench and bar about what civility means. A close reading of the Seventh Circuit Standards reveals that four basic concepts are the core of lawyer civility: courtesy, cooperation, honesty, and fair play.

Courtesy

Two of the Seventh Circuit standards relate to some form of courtesy. Under "Lawyer's Duties to Other Counsel," they provide that lawyers must "treat all other counsel, parties, and witnesses in a civil and courteous manner, not only in court, but also in all other written and oral communications." They further state that lawyers "will not, even when called upon by a client to do so, abuse or indulge in offensive conduct directed to other counsel, parties, or witnesses" and "will abstain from disparaging personal remarks or acrimony toward other counsel, parties, or witnesses" (Committee on Civility of the Seventh Federal Judicial Circuit 1992, 448–449).

We need to recognize at the outset that some conduct that normally would be condemned as discourteous is not considered uncivil for lawyers. A vigorous cross-examination may include aggressive questions, ridicule, sarcasm, and other time-honored rhetorical techniques for undermining credibility. For a memorable example, watch the cross-examination of William Jennings Bryan by Clarence Darrow in the movie, "Inherit the Wind." The discourtesy you see there is not uncivil as we define the term. It is discourteous in normal circumstances but has a legitimate purpose. But pointless rudeness certainly is uncivil. Examples abound.

Students are often surprised to learn that lawyers treat each other, and treat witnesses and parties, discourteously for no legitimate purpose. Sadly, they do. You can find a classic example of extreme discourtesy if you search YouTube for "old lawyer fight." Let's take a look at a few more examples.

Saldana v. Kmart Corp, 84 F. Supp. 2d 629 (D.V.I. 1999), is a vivid example of incivility as rudeness. In that case, the court sanctioned a lawyer for a number of comments. In a telephone deposition, the lawyer told opposing counsel, "Todd, I don't want to fuck around." In a later deposition, the lawyer told opposing counsel on the record, "I will put my remarks on the record as I'm entitled. I don't need to be lectured by you, sir. Don't fuck with me." In two conversations with attorneys, this lawyer made similar comments. She told one lawyer to "Just get me the fucking phone numbers" for an upcoming deposition and said to another, "You know Andy, go fuck yourself."

What happened in the *Saldana* case is not an isolated event. In its 2014 survey of Illinois lawyers, the Illinois Supreme Court Commission on Professionalism found that the most common type of uncivil or unprofessional conduct that lawyers experienced was some form of rudeness. Other examples are easy to find. Some of them, like the *Saldana* case, involve lawyers who are rude and intentionally insulting. The famous Texas lawyer Joe Jamail once told an opposing lawyer, "You could gag a maggot off a meat wagon." *Paramount Communications v. QVC Network*, 637 A.2d 34, 53 (Del. 1994). The insults have on occasion led beyond words. During a deposition, a lawyer "threw the contents of a soft drink cup on the plaintiff's attorney and grabbed him near or around his neck, restraining him in his chair." *In Re McClure*, 652 N.E.2d 863, 864 (Ind. 1995).

Other times the discourtesy is sexist or racist. In a 2007 survey, the Illinois Supreme Court Commission on Professionalism found that 52% of lawyers had experienced or witnessed sexist comments (Illinois Supreme Court Commission on Professionalism 2007). In one case, a male lawyer repeatedly called a female opposing counsel "hun" and "dear" during a deposition and talked about how she conducted the questioning "with your cute little thing going on." *Laddcap Value Partners, LP v. Lowenstein Sandler, P.C.*, 2007 WL 4901555 (Supreme Court of New York, New York County 2007). A lawyer used similar language in *Principe v. Assay Partners*, 586 N.Y.S.2d 182 (Supreme Court of New York, New York County 1992), when his comments included, "I don't have to talk to you, little lady"; "Tell that little mouse over there to pipe down"; "What do you know, young girl"; "Be quiet, little girl"; and "Go away, little girl." In another case, a male lawyer called his female opposing counsel "babe" but noted "[a]t least I didn't call you bimbo." *Mullaney v. Aude*, 730 A.2d 759 (Md. App. 1998).

In the 2007 Illinois survey, 42% of respondents had witnessed or experienced racist or culturally insensitive comments. As an example, read the following exchange between two opposing lawyers in a deposition:

MR. ROSEN: *You're not entitled to coach the witness any further, you're not entitled to.*

MR. WILLIAMS: *Don't use your little sheeny Hebrew tricks on me, Rosen.*

MR. ROSEN: *Off the record.*

MR. WILLIAMS: *No, on the record.*

MR. ROSEN: *You son of a bitch.*

MR. COX: *Let's call a recess.*

MR. ROSEN: *Tell the Judge I called him a rotten son of a bitch for calling me a sheeny Hebrew and I want to go see the Judge right now.*

IN RE WILLIAMS, 414 N.W.2D 394, 397–398 (MINN. 1987)

Discourtesy is not just a creature of lawyer-to-lawyer interactions. One lawyer threatened a pro se party that the lawyer would "rip his face off" if the pro se party disobeyed a court order. *Kalil's Case*, 773 A.2d 647 146 N.H. 466 (2001). Another lawyer made a point of lighting a lighter in front of an opposing party whose two children had died, allegedly as a result of the use of such a lighter. *Klemka v. Bic Corp.*, 1996 WL 103830 (E.D. Pa. 1996). Another threatened to shoot an opposing party and used a tractor bucket to lift and move that person's car approximately 200 feet. *In Re Beaver*, 181 Wis.2d 12, 17–19 (1994).

These examples illustrate that "civility" in the legal profession includes courtesy, a meaning that conforms to the common usage of the word. But civility for lawyers means more than just courtesy.

Cooperation

A second element of civility is cooperation with opposing counsel. Every professionalism and civility code or creed includes a plea for lawyers to cooperate with each other when the client's substantial rights are not at stake. The Seventh Circuit Standards, for example, include statements that lawyers will confer early about settlement, stipulate to undisputed matters, make good faith efforts to resolve objections by agreement, try to avoid scheduling conflicts and to accommodate other counsel's schedule, provide timely notice of the cancellation of events, agree to reasonable extensions of time, and draft and circulate for comments accurate proposed orders that reflect the court's rulings.

Lack of cooperation occurs most frequently in connection with scheduling arrangements for discovery and with respect to extensions of time. Although rules of civil procedure and other rules of court empower parties to initiate litigation events like depositions and hearings by giving appropriate notice, the practicalities of law practice and the many demands on a lawyer's time have made it customary for lawyers usually to work together to schedule events. Similarly, the rules of procedure set deadlines, but often lawyers agree to extend such deadlines when there is no prejudice to their clients.

We must recognize that sometimes the exigencies of the situation may mean that you should not be cooperative in the name of civility. Perhaps the opposing lawyer has asked for numerous extensions and/or the matter is time sensitive for your client. Civility does not require you to be a milquetoast. But the need for civility as cooperation appears most frequently in pointless posturing over routine matters.

The inability of lawyers to cooperate sometimes reaches absurd levels. The judge in *Avista Management, Inc. v. Wausau Underwriters Insurance Company* had heard enough about a disagreement over the location for a deposition and entered the following order:

> [T]he Court will fashion a new form of alternative dispute resolution, to wit: at 4:00 P.M. on Friday, June 30, 2006, counsel shall convene at a neutral site agreeable to both parties. If counsel cannot agree on a neutral site, they shall meet on the front steps of the Sam M. Gibbons U.S. Courthouse, 801 North Florida Ave., Tampa, Florida 33602. Each lawyer shall be entitled to be accompanied by one paralegal who shall act as an attendant and witness. At that time and location, counsel shall engage in one (1) game of "rock, paper, scissors." The winner of this engagement shall be entitled to select the location for the 30(b)(6) deposition to be held somewhere in Hillsborough County during the period July 11–12, 2006. If either party disputes the outcome of this engagement, an appeal may be filed and a hearing will be held at 8:30 A.M. on Friday, July 7, 2006 before the undersigned in Courtroom 3, George C. Young United States Courthouse and Federal Building, 80 North Hughey Avenue, Orlando, Florida 32801.

(Avista Management, Inc. v. Wausau Underwriters Insurance Company 2006, 1). The court's exasperation arose from the common understanding that lawyers need to cooperate with each other, when they can do so without harming their clients, if litigation is to proceed smoothly. "Civility" for lawyers includes this component of cooperation.

Honesty

A third element that permeates civility codes and creeds is the need for honesty, particularly with respect to agreements between opposing counsel and in the drafting of court orders. The Seventh Circuit Standards provide that lawyers "will adhere to all express promises and to agreements with other counsel, whether oral or in writing, and will adhere in good faith to all agreements implied by the circumstances or local customs." They also require lawyers who reduce an oral agreement to writing to do so accurately, to provide opposing counsel a chance to review the writing, and to alert opposing counsel to all changes made in any draft. The Standards also state that lawyers must not "falsely hold out the possibility of settlement as a means to adjourn discovery or to delay trial" (Committee on Civility of the Seventh Federal Judicial Circuit 1992, 449).

The need for these standards emerged from the survey that led to them. Things have apparently not changed. In the 2014 survey of Illinois lawyers, among the most frequent type of uncivil or unprofessional conduct that lawyers described experiencing in the previous six months was "misrepresenting or stretching the facts, or negotiating in bad faith" (National Center for Professional and Research Ethics 2014, 5).

In *Fire Ins. Exch. v. Bell*, 643 N.E.2d 310 (Ind. 1994), the court dealt with alleged misrepresentations by one lawyer to another and invoked the Seventh Circuit Standards and the Indianapolis Bar Association Tenets of Professional Courtesy. The litigation involved a fire at a home, and the lawyer for the homeowner's insurance company represented to plaintiff's counsel that the policy limits were $100,000 when in fact the policy limits were $300,000. Based upon opposing counsel's misrepresentation, and without exercising the right to formal discovery of the insurance policy, the plaintiff's lawyer recommended settlement for $100,000. When the truth emerged in later litigation against another party, the plaintiff sued the insurance company for fraud in connection with the negotiated settlement of the first case. The insurance company defended and argued that the plaintiff's attorney "had, as a matter of law, no right to rely on the alleged misrepresentations because he was a trained professional involved in adversarial settlement negotiation and had access to the relevant facts…" The court rejected this argument and held that lawyers have the right as a matter of law to rely upon the statements of other lawyers.

The opinion in *Fire Ins. Exch. v. Bell* involved affirmative misrepresentations. But the expectation of honesty, as a matter of civility, goes well beyond the avoidance of fraud. The court quoted the Indianapolis Tenets of Professional Courtesy, which state that "A lawyer … should always act pursuant to the maxim, 'My word is my bond.'" That maxim appears in numerous other civility codes and creeds. "Civility" for lawyers includes a sense of honor and truthfulness.

Fair play

The Seventh Circuit Guidelines go further than many codes and creeds of professionalism by setting forth detailed expectations about strategies that lawyers should restrain themselves from employing in civil litigation. Cases and commentary on this subject refer variously to some tactics as "hardball" or "Rambo" tactics that are employed to harass the opposing side or delay the resolution of a case. Surveys of lawyers about civility are replete with references to litigation "abuses," particularly in discovery. Here are some of the things that lawyers listed as civility problems for the survey that preceded promulgation of the Seventh Circuit standards:

Lawyers tend to drag out discovery and allow clients to respond slowly and incompletely necessitating motions to compel with or without sanctions. Judges dislike these motions because they perceive the attorneys as being able to resolve their difficulty without the judge. The judges' lack of patience with the attorneys, who by now are furious with each other, often results in arbitrary decisions by judges, making all parties frustrated and undermining the rational decision making process.

Lawyers attempting to gain unfair advantage on routine matters and playing "hardball."

Refusal to answer interrogatories and produce documents; playing "hard ball" at depositions; forcing unnecessary motions rather than cooperating voluntarily.

Hard-ball/hard-nose deposition tactics mainly. Also, some attorneys have a hair trigger when it comes to seeking or threatening sanctions.

(Committee on Civility of the Seventh Federal Judicial Circuit 1991, 386–388)

In the 2007 Illinois survey, 74% of responding lawyers reported experiencing other lawyers engaging in the indiscriminate or frivolous use of pleadings or motions. The 2014 follow-up survey found that over 11% of the respondents had experienced this tactic in the six months before the survey.

There is no shortage of reported cases lamenting lawyers' lack of restraint in using every available tactic to impede and delay an adversary, especially in discovery. The Supreme Court of Mississippi quoted the Mississippi Lawyer's Creed in its entirety in an interlocutory appeal of a discovery dispute for which the parties filed thousands of pages of exhibits. *Miss. Farm Bureau Mut. Ins. Co. v. Parker*, 921 So. 2d 260 (2005). In another case, the court noted that the parties had filed 19 motions regarding discovery tactics (more than half of which were filed in a single month) and had filed ten motions for sanctions. *Jaen v. Coca-Cola*, 157 F.R.D. 146, 148 (D. Puerto Rico 1994). Our electronic search for cases that discuss "hardball" tactics yielded a list of over 600 cases, while a search for "Rambo" was interrupted because it would retrieve more than 3,000 cases. *See, e.g., Canady v. Erbe Elektromedizin GmbH*, 307 F. Supp. 2d 2 (D.D.C. 2004) ("[t]his patent matter presents a textbook example of how Rambo-style litigation tactics prevent the just and speedy determination of a case").

Courtesy, cooperation, and truthfulness are universally recognized components of "civility" for lawyers. Although fair play is not always included, there is sufficient evidence from codes such as the Seventh Circuit Standards and from the courts to include it within our definition of civility. As you enter practice, you should be on the lookout for conduct that violates this definition of civility for lawyers.

WHAT CAUSES LAWYERS TO BE UNCIVIL?

If incivility impedes the profession's ability to fulfill its purposes, then it is crucial to understand why lawyers engage in it. A deep understanding of the various causes of incivility will help prepare you to deal with pressures and temptations to deviate from civility and will also help prepare you to understand and deal with the incivility of others.

Strategic incivility

Strategic incivility arises from a deliberate decision to be uncivil. The 2007 survey of Illinois lawyers found that deliberate strategic incivility is widespread and "includes misrepresenting or stretching facts, playing hardball, indiscriminate use of pleadings or motions, etc." (Illinois Supreme Court

Commission on Professionalism 2007, 11). In other words, strategic incivility is the deliberate disregard of all of the components of lawyer civility.

Lawyers who choose to employ incivility as a strategy perceive that it helps them succeed. We note right away that we do not concede this point in all circumstances. In fact, there are many who believe that civility is generally the more effective strategy. The perception, however, must be real, or lawyers who are driven to win would not use incivility as a weapon. What do they think they accomplish by deploying it?

One clue may lie in the finding in the 2007 Illinois survey that young lawyers encounter unprofessional conduct at relatively high levels. All types of incivility can be distracting and infuriating, but they are especially so when one has not encountered them before. For example, we have seen cases in which experienced lawyers have chosen to demean, insult, rant, or rave during depositions with young lawyers for the purpose of being distracting and infuriating. A distracted and infuriated lawyer is a less effective lawyer. Cool strategic thinking becomes much harder when an adversary makes your head spin and your blood boil. That type of distraction is the primary goal of the lawyer who employs strategic incivility.

Client expectations and increased competition

Two other causes of incivility that emerge from surveys of lawyers are very clear: clients want their lawyers to be unpleasant to their adversaries, and lawyers feel economic pressure to give in to those expectations.

It is understandable, and forgivable, for clients to want their lawyers to be unpleasant to the other side. Clients who are in litigation by definition have an adversary and most bear some ill will. They may want a lawyer who will channel that anger and act out on their behalf. It is this emotional state that some lawyers seek to exploit by advertising themselves as "pit bulls" or other various kinds of vicious animals. A lawyer who attracts business in this way will feel pressure to deliver. Note the possible but not inevitable overlap with strategic incivility. Lawyers who engage in strategic incivility do it in part to succeed economically and to attract and keep clients. As we described above, this is because they believe that incivility works. Lawyers who pander to client expectations of nastiness also act for economic reasons, and they might do it in part because they think it works. But they may also do it simply to keep the client happy, regardless of whether it makes victory more likely. These lawyers sometimes just make a preening show of nastiness for angry clients.

But surely clients have always wanted their lawyers to be nasty to their adversaries. Why would modern lawyers be more prone to meet or even feed those expectations? The answer lies in the sense of increasing economic competition that lawyers have been experiencing.

The 2007 Illinois survey found that economic pressures had the greatest influence on unprofessional behavior. The earlier survey conducted by the Seventh Circuit Committee on Civility directly asked lawyers several open-ended questions designed to solicit lawyers' views of the causes of incivility. A look at a few of the lawyers' comments helps to explain what is behind it.

The law profession is now a competitive business with enormous pressures on lawyers to meet large payrolls and carry a large overhead. I have found a "kill or be killed" attitude between lawyers who will probably never see an opposing counsel in another case. Clients also seem to want lawyers who take the "Rambo" approach and lawyers give in to this pressure.

> *I'm not sure when the change began to occur. Some lawyers were always difficult, but over the last 5–10 years, more lawyers seem to lack civility. The sheer numbers of lawyers now practicing and the pressure they get from clients certainly contributes. Also, they may start out being civil and professional and then see other lawyers succeed by using hard ball tactics and beings s.o.b.s, so they begin using these tactics.*
>
> *(Committee on Civility of the Seventh Federal Judicial Circuit 1991, 392)*

Lawyers who are fueled by a sense of desperate economic competition will be more tempted to use any means available to secure and keep clients, including the adoption of uncivil tactics.

Lack of formal or informal sanctions for incivility

Lawyers are under pressure to be uncivil, and many succumb because there is little reason to fear that they will suffer any consequences for doing so. As the cases we discussed earlier in the chapter show, a few courts have by order or through the exercise of their inherent power sanctioned lawyers for incivility. There are a few states that have found ways to discipline lawyers for extreme incivility for violating their oaths as lawyers, or violating a rule of conduct (not from the Model Rules), that require lawyers to "treat with courtesy and respect all others involved in the legal process." But formal sanctions for incivility, especially for behavior that is unreasonable but not outrageous, remain rare.

Lawyers encounter informal sanctions in some contexts but not others. For example, incivility is much more common in big cities than in smaller cities or towns. It is less common in highly specialized practice area where the attorneys have frequent interactions with each other. Why should the size of the community matter? The answer is simple and intuitive. When a lawyer chooses to behave with incivility, there may be informal consequences. Some of those can be personal. Lawyers do not want to socialize with lawyers who treat them shabbily. Other consequences are professional. A lawyer who knows from experience that a particular opposing counsel engages in uncivil conduct will be on guard the next time. One of our local judges likes to talk about his "list" of lawyers who have been uncivil. As he says, "you can move up the list, you can move down the list, but you never, ever come off the list." Lawyers who anticipate such informal consequences know that they will pay a price for uncivil conduct and are less prone to engage in it.

But those consequences become less likely in larger settings with more lawyers. The larger the pool of lawyers, the smaller the chances that one lawyer will repeatedly encounter another lawyer. Bigger cities will tend to have more lawyers. Less specialized practice areas have more lawyers. The informal costs of incivility are lower. If you're never going to see this other lawyer again, you need not fear being on his or her "list." Succumbing to the pressure or temptation to be uncivil is easier if the lawyer need not fear informal sanctions for doing so.

Reflexive or retaliatory incivility

Some incivility is the understandable response of a competitive person, in a situation of high-stakes conflict, to a perceived provocation. Texas attorney Mark Perlmutter has written a book with the title, *Why Lawyers (and the Rest of Us) Lie and Engage in Other Repugnant Behavior* (Perlmutter 1998). Perlmutter argues that a lack of self-awareness can lead us—lawyers and non-lawyers alike—to engage in shrill, unproductive and escalating conflict, particularly when we feel we have been provoked. Here is his description:

> *Hostile actions toward opposing lawyers virtually never produce submission. Many of us are lawyers precisely because we never want to appear weak. Such actions lead, instead, to escalation. Since most lawyers start out playing the "win/lose" game assumption, any show of hostility reinforces that assumption and triggers the provocation/response dynamic. Second, the message within each response is "I'll show you not to mess with me by hitting you **harder** than you hit me." As a young lawyer, I was told to give other lawyers the benefit of the doubt, but if they "crossed the line"—that is, did something unfair—my superiors advised me to bar no holds.*
>
> *Escalation, with lawyers, occurs in the "weapons" they use. If the other side has it, we must trump it…. Escalation occurs not only in weaponry but in tactics and emotion. Each new provocation calls for a more extreme response. Judges recognize these disputes when they feel the urge to tell the lawyers to "go to your rooms." Lawyers know they are in the midst of such an escalatory spiral when all they can think of at bedtime is, "How can I get back at that S.O.B.?"*
>
> (Perlmutter 1998, 53–54)

Put another way, incivility tends to beget more incivility. Lawyers who would never engage in strategic incivility, or who would never pander to client expectations of rudeness, find themselves screaming at opposing counsel in a deposition because the other side started it and they are not going to back down. Or, as one of us in practice had an unfortunate tendency to do, that lawyer may find himself brooding alone in his office, just thinking of things to do to the other lawyer as payback for a provocation. Scheming or brooding, this lawyer is engaging in reflexive or retaliatory incivility that is likely to escalate the situation. Tit for tat.

Lack of (or the wrong kind of) mentoring

We noted in Chapter 3 on competence that the legal profession's long tradition of older lawyers mentoring young lawyers has been eroding. That trend also affects civility, in that younger lawyers have less guidance about how to conduct themselves and how to deal with the incivility of others.

The effects of the decline in mentoring on civility may be worse than just a lack of positive influence on young lawyers. An experienced lawyer who chooses to engage in uncivil conduct sets an example. Whether the incivility is strategic, or results from a "win at all costs" mentality resulting from economic pressure, or comes from any other source, that conduct sends a profound message to new entrants into the profession. Young lawyers long to be "real" lawyers, and they often imprint the conduct that they first see from practicing lawyers. They may perceive that "toughness" and "hardball" are what the firm and the profession expect of them. In this sense, incivility may breed incivility from one generation to the next, as new entrants learn the wrong lessons from their seniors. These young lawyers are more likely to choose to be uncivil themselves, because they come to believe that this is what "real lawyers" do.

The general decline of civility in our society

Some lawyers believe that incivility occurs because some people are just "jerks." That, sadly, is true in our experience. But there is another cause of increasing incivility, one that would cause the prevalence of such people to expand. Increasing incivility is a social problem much wider than the legal profession, and lawyer incivility is merely a reflection of that degradation of societal norms of acceptable conduct. One judge observed in the Report for the Seventh Circuit:

> Today our talk is coarse and rude, our entertainment is vulgar and violent, our music is hard and loud, our institutions are weakened, our values are superficial, egoism has replaced altruism and cynicism pervades. Amid these surroundings none should be surprised that the courtroom is less tranquil. Cardozo reminds us that "judges are never free from the feelings of the times…"
>
> (Committee on Civility of the Seventh Federal Judicial Circuit 1992, 445)

The Seventh Circuit committee concluded that "these observations are apt and are no doubt contributing factors to the civility problems plaguing our profession."

Former Yale law school dean Anthony Kronman has echoed this argument:

> Is the spirit of civility dying in America? Many people think so. They say that our public discourse has become intemperate and mean; that tolerance and generosity are now rare in political debate; that the process of lawmaking is increasingly dominated by a ruthless partisanship whose expressions are barely distinguishable from physical violence; that candidates today ignore their opponents' ideas and attack their personalities instead, with ad hominem arguments of the cruelest and least charitable kind; that our whole public life has become degraded and harsh. The symptoms of this, they say, are visible wherever we look: in the venomous provocations of radio talk show hosts; in the lewd curiosities of the tabloid press; in the personal assaults that today pass for campaign advertising; in the sarcasm and anger of political argument generally.
>
> (Kronman 1995–1996, 727)

Note that both of these comments on a wider culture of incivility were made over 20 years ago. Some would no doubt argue that the societal trend toward incivility has only accelerated in the past 20 years. A lawyer in a November 2016 deposition was asked to stop saying insulting things. The lawyer responded, "At this point in time, a man who insults on a daily basis everybody he does business with has now been elected president of the United States. The standards have changed. I'll say what I want" (Rubino 2019). To cite another example, the prevalence of the internet and social media has increased the intemperance and meanness of our public and private conversations. On the other hand, these comments may be examples of the age-old phenomenon of older persons looking back nostalgically on an earlier era that was better than the present. It is clear from the survey results that jerks have always been with us. What is suspected, but not provable, is that we live in a time of more and more jerks.

STRATEGIES FOR CULTIVATING A DISPOSITION TOWARD CIVILITY

We are sorry to have to report to you that you almost certainly will encounter incivility in the practice of law. We wish this were not so. The experience is unpleasant and, for a new lawyer, can be disheartening. Here we offer some suggestions for how to deal with incivility when you run across it in order to help you implement a resolve to conduct yourself with civility.

Begin practicing courtesy and cooperation in law school

You are already in a competitive environment. Some students experience the temptation to be uncivil to classmates in various ways. Although it happens rarely, we have seen students who were needlessly contentious in classroom discussions and heard about students who did not cooperate with classmates for fear of losing an edge. These are precursors to uncivil conduct as a lawyer. Our students recite a creed during orientation, part of which is "To my fellow students, I offer my support, my respect, and my courtesy. I will strive to make our association a collegial one, in which we may depend upon each other for the benefit of all." One way to begin to cultivate a disposition toward civility as a lawyer is to take these words to heart and conduct yourself with civility now, while you are still in law school.

Do not be surprised, angered, or distracted

Now that you know that some incivility is strategic and has as its purposes to anger and distract you, you are better equipped to counteract it. When you encounter such conduct, take a deep breath and remember that you learned that this day was going to come. Remember that the strategic incivility only succeeds if you allow it to succeed. With patience and tenacity, stay focused and on task. You may find that the offending lawyer will stop engaging in such conduct once he or she knows that it is not going to work. That kind of lawyer is testing you. You can pass the test by demonstrating equanimity rather than anger or distraction.

Observe the formalities

Lawyer cooperation is so important in part because if every case had to proceed "by the book" the entire system would likely collapse of its own weight. But remember in extreme circumstances that there is "a book"—the rules of procedure. This strategy may be particularly necessary if you are dealing with someone who is acting like a jerk because he or she is a jerk. If such a lawyer refuses to return a phone call to give you a date for a deposition of his client, send a notice. If a lawyer engages in hardball tactics by sending oppressive discovery and will not consider any compromise, file a motion for protective order. When a lawyer yells at you in a deposition to "move on," stand your ground and insist on an answer from the witness. For the lawyer who shows a willingness to lie, insist on all communications being in writing. Your protection ultimately may lie in your deep knowledge of and facility with the rules of procedure. Use them when civility fails.

Make the record

Although many judges are loath to hear complaints from lawyers about the incivility of opposing counsel, you must be prepared either to present or defend against such complaints. Again, making sure that communications are in writing is crucial. Be sure to video all depositions so that you have a record that will capture not just the words that are said but also the tone with which they are uttered. Write confirming letters when oral agreements have been reached. Be sure that all of your communications are supremely professional, so that a judge who someday has occasion to read them will be impressed. Keep meticulous records of all communications with opposing counsel, including any that come by text or by social media. You usually do not want to have a hearing about civility with a judge, but in case you do have one do not go unarmed.

Refuse to be provoked

Remember that the cause of much incivility is provocation by the opposing lawyer. If you allow yourself to be provoked, the other lawyer wins. You are not doing your best job of representing your client when you focus on responding to every slight and escalating incivility started by the other lawyer. You also will have a very tough time if the disputes ever end up in front of a judge, because the judge is not going to be interested when you say, "but he started it." The judge at best will see two uncivil lawyers, like two scorpions in a bottle, and treat you and the provocateur with equal disgust. Don't get mad. Don't get even. Don't give in to the temptation to show how tough you are. If you find it therapeutic, write a nasty letter or email. Just don't send it. Stay focused on representing your client's interests.

Clarify and manage supervisor expectations

As we have mentioned, sometimes young lawyers act uncivilly because they watch older lawyers misbehave and think that this is what "real" lawyers do. They want to meet what they perceive to be the expectations of their new employers. The first bit of advice is to try to detect in the interviewing process what the firm's attitude toward civility is. If you hear "Rambo litigator" used as a compliment, for example, you may want to re-think whether that is the firm for you. If you are already employed, then you need to try to clarify the expectations of the firm. With luck, you may learn that you misunderstood or misconstrued the signals the firm was sending you. On the other hand, it is possible that you were right, and that the firm expects you to practice without regard to your duty of civility. We hope you are never in this position, but if you are then you will have a choice to make. As we discussed in Chapter 2, one thing to keep in mind is that your satisfaction as a lawyer is going to be tied directly to the components of your professional identity. A lawyer whose professional identity includes a commitment and disposition to civility is more likely to find meaning and satisfaction in the profession. In the long run, you will be better off if you stick to your commitment to civility and, if necessary, find another job.

Manage client expectations

As you develop professionally, you will eventually be in a position to manage the expectations of clients who may want to hire you to be nasty and uncivil to the other side. This is time for a frank discussion with your would-be client. Comment 6 to Model Rule of Professional Conduct 1.2 provides a partial guide: "[T]he terms upon which representation is undertaken may exclude specific means that might otherwise be used to accomplish the client's objectives." You can explain that you understand the client's anger and inclination to a scorched-earth strategy, but you should also explain that the best way for you to help the client is for you to conduct yourself in the way the courts and the profession expect you to. That means, among other things, that you will be courteous and cooperative with the client's adversary. If you are not, then the cost of the matter will increase enormously, because litigating "by the book" is much more expensive than being civil. You can also explain that the most important asset you can deploy in your client's interest is your credibility, which you have nurtured by conducting yourself appropriately in prior cases. It is part of what the client is paying you for. You should make clear to the client that you have obligations to the opposing lawyer and party and to the court and that you intend to comply with those obligations. This is a great time to secure an understanding from the client that this is how you practice law and, if the client wants you, it is how you are going to handle the matter.

CONCLUSION

Civility is one of the six virtues of the professional lawyer. It is necessary in order for lawyers to fulfill their public purposes and to serve their clients well. In this chapter, we have attempted to sensitize you to what civility means and why lawyers sometimes act uncivilly. We have also tried to provide some guidance on how to implement a disposition toward civility, despite the obstacles you will encounter in practice.

DISCUSSION QUESTIONS AND PROBLEMS

1   Suppose you are handling a case against a contentious lawyer. You file a motion with the court and allege that opposing counsel made a mistake in how he handled the case. The opposing lawyer sends you a text message that says, "I'm handling more than 200 cases, many of which are more important/significant than the little claims that are handled by bottom feeding/scum sucking/loser lawyers like yourself." How do you respond? This is a real case. Research it and find out what happened next. Reflect on how a different response might have led to a better result.

2   Suppose you are a transactional lawyer. One of your fellow associates is working on a deal and receives the following voicemail from a lawyer on the other side of the deal. Reflect on why the lawyer who left this message would have handled himself this way. Counsel your fellow associate about what to do next.

> We got your last message. I'll tell you very bluntly. If you are intending in any way to send these emails for any purpose whatsoever other than to vent, my response to you is very simply going to be save your fucking breath. And if you have any issue ... call us and discuss them. If you send one more fucking email like this again, I can assure you your life on this deal is going to be very unpleasant because I'm gonna get my client involved and we're going to make it very clear that you are not cooperating. ... You made a change without our authorization. Whether you consider it material or not, again, I don't give a flying fuck. Make the fucking change. Be the middleman monkey, or give us the job to

do and we'll take care of it and we'll do it properly. Your mortgage document was sloppy and shitty. All right. ... If you can't be a monkey fucking scribe, then you know what – let us do it. We'll get one of our secretaries to handle it.

This was a real voicemail. Research it and listen to it for yourself. Reflect on how you would have felt if you had received it. What would you have been tempted to do immediately? On reflection?

3   You have a new client, a physician who is accustomed to being in charge of things. The doctor is involved in civil litigation with a former business partner. At the outset of the case, your client instructs you to conduct the case "by the book" and not to cooperate in any way with the opposing counsel except as required under the rules. The doctor tells you, "I know how you lawyers work—you scratch each other's backs while the clients pay, but not this time—they wanted a war, and we are going to give it to them." How do you respond to your client? What do you anticipate your client's response will be?

4   You are a new associate at a civil litigation firm. You accompany your supervising lawyer to a deposition, where you watch her berate and intimidate a young lawyer who is defending the deposition. The other lawyer is so flustered by the experience that he fails to make several relevant objections. After you leave the deposition, your supervisor tells you, "see—that's how it's done. If you sense weakness, exploit it. Don't be a jerk just to be a jerk, but if being a jerk will help the client, then have at it." How would you respond to your supervisor? What effect would this experience have on your future conduct?

5   You are litigating a case in which one of your good friends from law school is opposing counsel. Your friend calls to tell you that he accidentally neglected to identify a crucial expert witness as part of a pretrial order in your case. If the expert does not testify, your client certainly will win the case. Your friend asks you, as just a "small favor," not to object at the hearing when he offers the expert. Your friend reminds you of "how important all the judges say civility is" and then offers to help you prepare to cross-examine the expert successfully. What are your options in responding to your friend? Which option would you choose?

REFERENCE LIST AND SUGGESTED READINGS

Avista Management, Inc. v. Wausau Underwriters Insurance Company. 2006. *Order of the Court.* http://archive.fortune.com/2006/06/07/magazines/fortune/judgerps_fortune/index.htm.

Burger, Warren E. 1971. The Necessity for Civility, Remarks of the Honorable Warren E. Burger, Chief Justice of the United States at the Opening Session – American Law Institute. *Federal Rules Decisions* 52:211.

Carter, Stephen L. 1999. *Civility: Manners, Morals and the Etiquette of Democracy.* New York: Basic Books.

Committee on Civility of the Seventh Federal Judicial Circuit. 1992. Final Report. *Federal Rules Decisions* 143:441.

Committee on Civility of the Seventh Federal Judicial Circuit. 1991. Interim Report. *Federal Rules Decisions* 143:371.

Grenardo, David A. 2013. Making Civility Mandatory: Moving from Aspired to Required. *Cardozo Public Law Policy & Ethics Journal* 11:239.

Illinois Supreme Court Commission on Professionalism. 2007. *Survey on Professionalism.* www.2civility.org/wp-content/uploads/2013/12/surveyonprofessionalism_final.pdf.

Kronman, Anthony T. 1995–1996. Civility. *Cumberland Law Review* 26:727.

National Center for Professional and Research Ethics. 2014. *Survey on Professionalism: A Study of Illinois Lawyers* 2014. www.2civility.org/wp-content/uploads/2015/04/Study-of-Illinois-Lawyers-2014.pdf.

O'Connor, Sandra Day. 1998. Professionalism. *Washington University Law Quarterly* 76:5.

Perlmutter, Mark. 1998. *Why Lawyers (and the Rest of Us) Lie and Engage in Other Repugnant Behavior*. Cambridge: Bright Books.

Reavely, Thomas M. 1990. Rambo Litigators: Pitting Aggressive Tactics against Legal Ethics. *Pepperdine Law Review* 17:637.

Rubino, Kathryn. 2019. Attorney Calls Opposing Counsel a "B*tch" – Justifies Outrageous Behavior Because Trump. *Above the Law*. https://abovethelaw.com/2019/01/attorney-calls-opposing-counsel-a-btch-justifies-outrageous-behavior-because-trump/.

8

PRACTICAL WISDOM
AS A PROFESSIONAL VIRTUE

INTRODUCTION

So far, we've made the case that your journey to becoming a lawyer should involve forming the kind of professional identity that will allow you to act effectively and ethically as a lawyer and to live a life of well-being and satisfaction. Achieving that end requires that you cultivate the first five lawyerly virtues and integrate them with your own personal values. Those are big tasks, but accomplishing them will not be enough. It is the sixth virtue—practical wisdom—that will enable you to put it all together in the many moments of professional practice that await you as a lawyer.

Do not underestimate how difficult this will be. You've undertaken the difficult, but worthwhile, commitment to become a professional. That means that you will be called upon to exercise judgment under conditions of inherent uncertainty and to do so in your capacity as a fiduciary for your client. Sometimes, you will have time for thoughtful reflection about what the desired action or outcome is, including time to consult with others, but at other times you may be called upon to live out your professional goals and obligations almost immediately upon learning of the dilemma to which you are responding.

Sometimes you will be called upon to decide between ethically and morally right and wrong choices. But in many moments of your life as a lawyer, the toughest decisions will be choosing the best among a set of actions, all of which are ethical and moral, that accomplish your or your client's goals to a greater or lesser degree. And once you decide *what* to do, you must decide on *how* to do it. All of the lawyerly virtues and your personal values may be in play simultaneously. How do you make sure that you are employing all of them in the right mix in the right way for the right reasons at any given moment? The answer is to exercise the sixth virtue, practical wisdom.

WHAT IS PRACTICAL WISDOM?

Practical wisdom is an ancient concept, and many trace its roots to Aristotle. When Aristotle wrote about practical wisdom, he wasn't applying it in the context of professional actions, but more broadly. He argued that practical wisdom is the virtue that allows the best application of many characteristics, such as loyalty, self-control, courage, fairness, generosity, gentleness, friendliness, and truthfulness.

Modern writers have also written about practical wisdom, including its importance in professional practice. In a recent book, Schwartz and Sharpe tell us that practical wisdom is "the right way to do the right thing in a particular circumstance, with a particular person, at a particular time" (Schwartz and Sharpe 2010, 5–6). Note what they are emphasizing here: wisdom is needed to understand the specific context in which any ethical action is taken. Wisdom is often thought of as philosophical or abstract reasoning, but the adjective "practical" tells us that it means something different here. *Practical* wisdom is the ability to implement the right action in particular circumstances. Hence, the wisdom is applied (or practical), which means that it is specific to a particular context.

When you have practical wisdom, you are able to draw upon general rules and knowledge, as well as general skills, but to do so in a way that recognizes that each situation is unique. A person with practical wisdom uses past experience with similar situations and will know that no two situations are exactly the same; she will adapt to the dissimilarities of each situation while recognizing the similarities between the present and past ones. Practical wisdom requires constant movement between the general and the particular.

You've no doubt engaged in the kind of process that leads to practical wisdom in your personal life, most likely in situations involving your family or friends. For example, you may have had to achieve the right balance between honesty and kindness when a friend proudly prepared a new recipe for you, which you didn't find appealing. Did you tell him the truth about how you thought it tasted, or did you moderate your review because you knew that your friend had worked hard on the meal and was particularly sensitive to criticism? If you did offer some criticism, did you offer it in the way that this friend would best receive it—did you do so jokingly, or by offering a helpful critique as a mentor/teacher would? Would your reaction have been different if there were others present, so that your honest assessment had the potential to embarrass your friend as well as hurt his feelings? What if the meal contained an ingredient to which you have a severe allergy? Your wisdom may have helped you have the courage to tell the friend unwelcome news in order to protect your health, but do it in the right way for this particular friend and in that particular situation.

In your professional life, you will use the personal values and skills that you have accumulated through your life and integrate them with the professional virtues and skills that you are acquiring. You will build upon your developing practical wisdom acquired through your life so far. The task becomes more complex in the professional setting, both because you are bringing to bear a new set of considerations and because you are acting as a fiduciary, setting aside self-interest in favor of your obligations to your client, and simultaneously respecting your duties to the law and the public interest. Practical wisdom helps you to resolve tensions among the influences on your actions, including but not only the other five lawyer virtues, and to recognize when you might be overemphasizing a particular virtue to the potential neglect of another.

Let's look at a couple of examples. Suppose that you are in the midst of a toughly-negotiated real estate deal in which your client wants to sell a valuable piece of property. You then learn that your client had misstated a fact about the property in a letter to the buyer. What do you do? You must apply the virtue of fidelity to the client, including the duties of loyalty and of attorney-client confidentiality, in a way that also applies the virtue of fidelity to the law.

Fidelity to the client alone might incline you to keep quiet, unless it is in your client's interest to reveal the mistake. Generally, information such as what you have learned about the error is confidential and must remain so because it relates to your representation. Your duty of loyalty will require you to explore the client's interests and wishes, which may be some mix of a desire to get the deal done, to protect his reputation, or to be sure not to do something that he considers to be wrong. If the client wants to fix the error, the problem goes away. But if the client wants to proceed without revealing it, then you have other things to consider.

Your duty of fidelity to the law may be in play. The rules of professional conduct offer guidance. Rule 4.1(b) tells you when you must reveal confidential information in order to avoid assisting in a fraud. If this situation falls under that rule, then your duty is clear, although you have some flexibility in how you accomplish making sure the other side knows of the mistake. Fidelity to the law will trump fidelity to the client.

But the situation might not be so simple. If Rule 4.1(b) does not require you to tell, you can look to Rule 1.6 to see if this situation falls into one of the optional exceptions to your duty of confidentiality. If so, you'll have to decide whether you will choose to reveal the mistake. If you do not even have the option to reveal, your personal values might be telling you to withdraw because you think your client is doing a bad but not illegal thing.

This example illustrates why you will not find a disciplinary rule regarding practical wisdom and why lawyers generally enjoy "judgmental immunity" from malpractice claims for giving advice in unsettled circumstances. There is no one right answer.

It is practical wisdom that allows you to choose the best course of action in such particular circumstances when the law does not dictate your conduct. The exercise of practical wisdom will allow you to deploy all of the tools of the good lawyer in the best way. Without it, you might overemphasize one virtue and underemphasize another. Or, as Aristotle put it, you might have "too much" of one of the virtues—too much of the virtue of fidelity to the client and too little of fidelity to the law might result in not addressing the client's situation. Practical wisdom will allow you to determine and act upon the proper balance among them. It will also tell you the best way to do it. Do you talk to your client first and advise him that you and he should jointly reveal the error to the buyer? If you do, what tone will you take with your client? Do you accuse him of dishonesty or begin the conversation by being open to the possibility that he made an honest mistake? Is your plan to persuade him to reveal the information, or is it just to inform him of the fact that you intend to (or must) reveal it? Or, do you take one of the many other paths to resolving this dilemma? As with every other exercise of practical wisdom, all of these choices need to take into consideration the applicable rules, the lawyer virtues, and the particulars of this case.

Another example is that of a criminal defense lawyer who has received a plea offer for his client. The ethical lawyer knows that a plea offer, just like a settlement offer in a civil case, must be conveyed to the client and that the client, not the lawyer, makes the decision whether to accept it. Without recognizing and acting upon those fundamental rules of practice, the lawyer will violate basic professional standards and act unethically. But the lawyer's decision-making doesn't stop there, for there is a wide range of actions within the ethical choice to follow the rules. There are better and worse ways of conveying the offer to the client, and of counseling the client about the pros and cons of accepting the offer. The best lawyers, those who are practically wise, take into account such things as previous experience with other clients, knowledge of the judge who will have to approve the agreement, whether this prosecutor might be open to other options if the offer is refused, of how the client's life will be affected by different choices, and of the likely outcome if the offer is refused and the case is tried. The best lawyer will do so with an informed understanding of this particular client's needs, goals, personality, and ability to understand and communicate. The best lawyer has taken time to know what this particular client's concerns are—for example, is it more important to the client that he has his day in court or that those close to him not be required to testify? The best lawyer will know that the way she frames the choices to the client may affect the client's decision and will know that this client may have a different way of reacting or reasoning than the last client whom she counseled on a plea offer. And, of course, the best lawyer will be balancing tensions among the five lawyer virtues along with qualities such as kindness, empathy, and courage.

Practical wisdom is the "master virtue"

Practical wisdom is often called "the master virtue," meaning that it is the virtue that allows you to call upon all of the other virtues and to implement ethical action even in the midst of complex and uncertain situations. As the master virtue, it is the only virtue that you cannot have too much of. The other virtues are all essential, but if you overemphasize one to the exclusion of another (have "too much" of any particular one), you may not take the optimal action. Aristotle uses the virtue of generosity as an example. It is certainly possible not to be generous enough, but Aristotle points out that one can be too generous. Giving away everything you have is generous but would leave you with no way to support yourself or your family. There can be too much of a virtue—too much of a good thing—in particular situations.

Practical wisdom will help you apply the "right amount" of the lawyer virtues to take the best action. By characterizing practical wisdom as the master virtue, we are recognizing the complexity of the work you will do as a lawyer. You have to have a means of bringing many different things to bear at once, and practical wisdom is the virtue that allows you to do that.

Practical wisdom is the movement between the general and the particular

As we noted earlier in the chapter, practical wisdom requires constant movement between the general and the particular. It requires the application of general principles and rules to the particulars of the moment. That is what distinguishes practical wisdom from theoretical or philosophical wisdom. It is nuanced and contextual. It requires the lawyer to know the rules of professional conduct and the lawyer virtues, and to access personal and professional skills and values so that the best among a range of ethical actions is taken. It emphasizes the importance of exercising discretion or judgment. The constant moving between the general and the particular allows for both detached observation and analysis and also for empathetic understanding of and engagement with a particular person or situation. It has been described as "bifocal" for this reason.

Adapting to the particulars of a given situation may actually become more difficult as you gather experiences and expertise. When you are counseling a client early in your career, each encounter will seem like a new experience, allowing you to treat each uniquely and to focus on the specifics of the facts and the client's goals and needs. As you accumulate those experiences, it becomes more tempting to treat each one with a sort of shorthand and assume that each will be like some other. The temptation to think, for example, that "this is another married couple with a simple estate who need a will, and, therefore, I know that they need what the last ten married couples with a simple estate needed," becomes stronger. It requires greater commitment and intentionality to approach each as a new experience.

An experienced and highly successful lawyer once explained that he takes a few minutes before meeting each new client to "say goodbye before saying hello." He explained that what he meant was that he intentionally focuses on putting aside assumptions about the new situation based on having handled many similar cases in the past. He focuses on being open to listening for the particulars of this client's life and needs. It's not that he ignores the previous cases. He draws upon the expertise developed from accumulated experiences in similar cases. After all, that developed expertise is part of what makes him valuable to the client. Instead, he moves back and forth between the general and the particular, the hallmark of practical wisdom. To be able to do so, he has developed a habit that ensures that he does not overemphasize his past experience and underemphasize the uniqueness of this client's situation. That seemingly simple habit—saying good-bye before saying hello—allows him the opportunity to exercise practical wisdom, and this habit is an indication that he has acquired practical wisdom.

Practical wisdom is dependent upon other virtues

As the master virtue, practical wisdom is dependent upon the lawyer's having acquired other needed virtues and skills, some of which are professional and some of which are personal. These include such things as self-awareness, reflection, courage, empathy, and the five other lawyer virtues. In other words, practical wisdom is dependent upon your development of a professional identity that allows you to integrate the professional virtues and skills of a lawyer with your personal values and skills. You must be able to access multiple capacities at once to decide upon and implement the wisest decision under the circumstances.

The exercise of practical wisdom has been compared to the actions of a skilled jazz musician. Jazz is the epitome of improvisation, moving back and forth between a musical score and what is happening in the moment, of being able to read what other musicians are doing and respond. A novice jazz musician begins with the fundamental skills of musicianship. Without those, there is no bedrock for improvisation. Then he will develop various other skills over time and eventually, as he gains expertise, the improvisation will begin to happen reflexively, or automatically. That is because the musician has developed habits and dispositions of both musicianship and improvisation that can be called upon simultaneously to create beautiful music. Improvisation only happens because of the presence of other skills, just as practical wisdom occurs only if the lawyer has developed the right virtues and skills. Part of cultivating practical wisdom is continued attention to the other five lawyer virtues and personal characteristics.

An example is empathy. It is not strictly a professional characteristic, but as we have seen it is part of the lawyerly virtue of fidelity to the client. Empathy is essential to your being able to see the situation from the perspective of your client. It requires your having the moral imagination to understand what another person is feeling and to see the situation as the other person does. Therefore, the personal characteristic of empathy is a component of several professional virtues. You must be able to balance that empathy with a professional detachment and objectivity, and that is where practical wisdom fits in.

Similarly, practical wisdom is dependent upon an understanding of and commitment to the public aims of the profession. Lawyers, as do other professionals, contribute to society through their work, and as you know one of the six virtues is commitment to public service. Your ability to exercise practical wisdom is dependent upon your understanding and practice of that virtue. Practical wisdom is what allows lawyers to translate the public aims of the profession into concrete action on behalf of their clients and the legal system and in the public interest.

Practical wisdom's dependence upon other virtues is consistent with empirical research on how humans engage in ethical actions. You will recall the four component model of moral behavior described in Chapter 1. It teaches us that ethical action requires four things: *sensitivity* to the situation in which the ethical dilemma arises, the ability to *reason* to the ethical result, the *motivation* to act ethically, and the ability to *implement* the ethical action, even in the face of difficulty. The practically wise lawyer will recognize ethical dilemmas, know the difference between an ethical and unethical response, be motivated to act ethically, and have the right combination of character traits and skill to implement the best ethical action in the particular situation. Just as the four component model demonstrates that a deficiency of any one of the four will prevent ethical behavior, we know that practical wisdom is dependent upon the presence of all of the other lawyer virtues.

Practical wisdom is expert judgment

Practical wisdom as applied in professional life is what many people think of as expert judgment, or expertise. It is the distinctive skill that a lawyer offers to a client, and its exercise is a result of having developed a professional identity that integrates the lawyer's personal and professional values and that has assimilated the lawyer virtues. It has another role as well. Because lawyering is only done on behalf of someone else, the lawyer must know how to create the opportunity for others to exercise practical wisdom. The practically wise lawyer will help the client exercise practical wisdom. We earlier used an example of counseling a client about accepting a plea bargain offer. The practically wise lawyer will understand that the ways in which she presents the options to the client can affect whether the client is able to make a wise decision. The lawyer's actions are dependent upon the lawyer's having practical wisdom and also creating the opportunity for the client to exercise practical wisdom.

CHALLENGES TO PRACTICAL WISDOM

A culture of speed

Modern life moves fast. Modern forms of communication mean that lawyers are expected to reply instantaneously to client inquiries. Often the exercise of practical wisdom requires time to consider and reflect. Yet you will feel pressure to please your clients and to respond immediately with your advice. Sometimes that is fine, because the question is simple. Sometimes it is necessary, because the circumstances are urgent. But too often the client's sense of urgency and demands for an immediate response are unnecessary and dangerous. A complex problem with multiple conflicting goals and irreducible uncertainty is not something about which you should give advice in haste unless it is necessary to do so. Practical wisdom sometimes takes time.

The tyranny of rules

Schwartz and Sharpe, in their book on practical wisdom, argue that the modern world erodes practical wisdom through a dependence upon rules to control behavior (Schwartz and Sharpe 2010, 12, 113–128). Too many rules can eliminate discretion, which is necessary for practical wisdom. The good news is that many of the rules of professional conduct leave room for lawyer discretion. A lawyer may but need not reveal confidential information under the circumstances set forth in rules 1.6(b) and 1.13(c). The rules on conflicts of interest mostly call upon lawyers to make fact-specific judgments about circumstances that might impair their representation of a client. In all but one situation, a lawyer has discretion to decide whether or not to call as a witness someone whom the lawyer believes, but does not know, will offer false evidence. All of these situations leave room for practical wisdom.

But the life of the lawyer is not immune from this general trend toward controlling people with rules rather than allowing them to exercise judgment. Schwartz and Sharpe offer an example from the law: sentencing guidelines have eliminated much of the discretion that judges once had in imposing sentences upon convicted criminals. The guidelines arise from well-meaning intent for fairness, recognizing that those who commit the same crime should suffer the same punishment, a general approach that makes sense. Yet not all situations that look the same from the outside are actually the same. Historically, judges were able to exercise their discretion to recognize both the similarities and the dissimilarities between cases. It is the judge who knows the details of each situation. Practical wisdom can be exercised only if the judge is able to move back and forth between the general and the particular and to ask herself: what is the right sentence for this situation at this time? Without the ability to depart from sentencing guidelines, that question does not matter because each situation is treated as if it is similar to many others.

You should be attuned to situations in which rules circumscribe your ability to use your judgment. Firm or corporate policies of "zero tolerance" for certain kinds of behaviors are good examples. As an attorney, you will want to consider whether it would be better for your client or your employer to leave you with some discretion or to cabin you with rules. Remember that it is only practical wisdom that will enable you to take into account all the circumstances of a particular situation. Rules take away that freedom.

The corruption of incentives

In addition to rules, many settings offer incentives as a driver for human behavior. Schwartz and Sharpe identify this trend as well as a threat to practical wisdom (Schwartz and Sharpe 2010, 12, 177–196). The problem with undue reliance on incentives is that they have the potential to skew the delicate processes of practical wisdom. Take the example of a young lawyer working on a billable hour case. The lawyer needs to decide whether to research a particular issue that may be tangential to the client's matter. Competence (as diligence) would weigh in favor of doing the research. Fidelity to the client might for some clients weigh in favor of not doing so because the added expense might not be worth the speculative benefit of the research to the client. But the stakes for the client might be high. Or the client may be extremely cost sensitive. The lawyer exercises practical wisdom by charting a course that best balances the competing virtues and best serves the particular client.

Now add to the mix a billable hour incentive for the young lawyer. Suppose the firm promises a bonus at the end of the year if the lawyer exceeds 2,200 billable hours. We saw in Chapter 4 that as a lawyer you must have the mental discipline and moral fortitude to set aside personal interests and serve your client. Ideally, this young lawyer would do just that and ignore the prospect of the bonus. But the potential of the incentive to skew the lawyer's judgment is undeniable. There is temptation to reach for the incentive and do the extra research as a result of an exercise of "wisdom" that has been corrupted by a personal interest.

Incentives are not going to disappear from our personal or professional lives. The lesson is to be sufficiently self-aware that you are attentive to their influence on your life and resist the temptation to give them too much weight to the detriment of the things that truly matter. You must be sufficiently committed to the cultivation of practical wisdom that you don't allow incentives to prevent the right balance of the lawyer virtues in any given situation.

The dangers presented by incentives are a good time to remind you of the distinction we have made before between extrinsic and intrinsic motivations. The bonus for meeting the billable hour quota is an extrinsic motivation. What should be countering the incentive is the intrinsic motivation to do the job the right way, to make the decision about the extra work with the client's interests in mind because of the intrinsic rewards that come from being a certain kind of lawyer and a certain kind of person—the kind who puts others' needs before self-interest. And remember that acting from intrinsic motivations is much more powerfully associated with a sense of well-being than acting from an extrinsic motivation.

STRATEGIES FOR CULTIVATING PRACTICAL WISDOM

Practical wisdom develops over time, with experience. This book is about your transition from student to lawyer. That transition will happen as you accumulate new knowledge about the law and legal system, and about yourself, and as you gain experiences from which you can learn. The process of acquiring practical wisdom is happening simultaneously with the acquisition of the other lawyer virtues and with continued personal and professional growth in all areas. But, because practical wisdom is the virtue that regulates and allows you to implement all of the others in a complex situation, it is in some ways the hardest to develop. It takes the longest. You will not have fully developed the practical wisdom of the best lawyers upon your graduation from law school, but the process certainly can begin in school.

What does it take to become a practically wise lawyer? As with the old joke about how to get to Carnegie Hall, the answer is "practice, practice, practice." It takes experience, but experience alone will not do it. If it did, all people would acquire practical wisdom as they age. But they do not. Everyone gains experience as they move through life, but not everyone gains practical wisdom.

The acquisition of practical wisdom is a developmental process that takes intention and hard work. Law school, and your life experiences after graduation, will provide plenty of experience by which you can develop the practical wisdom you need as a lawyer. It will not happen automatically, though. That is because some experiences undermine wisdom and also because, even with the right kind of experiences, not everyone learns from them. You must use your experiences to learn so that you develop certain habits that will then allow you to act with practical wisdom in difficult and complex moments of professional practice. Developing these habits will create in you a disposition toward practical wisdom so that you can reflexively call upon your professional identity to best implement the right decision in the right way in any given situation.

The habit of reflection

One of the critical habits that you must develop is that of reflection. Educational research has demonstrated that humans do not learn through experience alone. When you have an experience, whether successful or unsuccessful, you should take the time to reflect upon the experience so that the next time you have a similar experience you will be informed by your reflection and be able to adapt what you do based on that reflection. There are two types of reflection that the best professionals habitually engage in: reflection in the midst of a situation and reflection after it is over. Both are essential.

When in the midst of doing something—interviewing a new client, for example—the practically wise lawyer will adjust throughout the interview to the client's reactions, emotions, unexpected answers, and many other things. The lawyer will begin the interview with a plan, perhaps a list of questions and areas to be discussed and some overall goals for the interview. The lawyer will adjust the original plan throughout the interview and adapt to the situation as it unfolds. That ability to adapt is dependent upon bringing to the interview many skills that have developed through lifetime experiences and of having acquired the lawyer virtues. The effective lawyer will be able to read the client's facial expressions and understand when an area of inquiry is upsetting. Depending upon the goal, she may leave that area and go to another less emotional area to give the client time to compose himself. Or the lawyer may see that the phrasing of a question is causing the client to withdraw a bit and hold back, so she does something to relieve the pressure of the situation, which she hopes will encourage the client to more open discussion. The lawyer's thinking in the moment causes her to reshape what she is doing even while she is doing it. It is a spontaneous and expert execution of the many skills and experiences that she brings to the situation, that is, of her professional identity. Sometimes, the reshaping is triggered by an unexpected moment, which we might characterize as a surprise. With accumulated experiences, even a surprise may be within a range of familiar experiences, but still requires that the lawyer adapt to it. Whether to something wholly unexpected, or to something that comes within a range of expected actions by the client, the practically wise lawyer will use her past experiences and the expertise gained from them to adapt to the particulars of the present. The surprise will trigger a moment of reflection that will then inform the lawyer's response.

The use of the term "reflection" may lead you to imagine the lawyer pausing and thinking deeply at each stage of such a process. That is not always so. The proper "reflection" may take place in a very short period of time, perhaps even seconds, and the lawyer who is skillful at this kind of reflection in the midst of the situation may not be not consciously aware of the complex processes that support it in the moment. She may not be able to describe it if asked about it afterwards. She may not be consciously aware that her action—whether it is a question or response or simply a facial expression—demonstrates a manifestation of the lawyer virtues. Yet she has developed the practical wisdom to reflexively employ the various skills and virtues of a good lawyer in the given situation. She has benefitted from her accumulated experience so that her thinking and doing are complementary actions. Her reflection benefits her action, even as it takes place in the context of the action.

Remember that this lawyer wasn't always able to do this. It is likely the case that in her early years as a lawyer, she was not the skillful interviewer she is today. She may not have picked up on the client's facial cues, or she may have responded in unhelpful ways when she did. She may have resolved the tension between the lawyer virtues in ways that overemphasized the wrong one, or she might have let self-interest affect her action. She has become the good lawyer that she is because she has used her experiences, both positive and negative, to develop the habit of adaptive reflection in the moment through repeated practice. She has formed a professional identity that allows her to demonstrate practical wisdom.

In addition to the habit of reflection and adaptation in the moment, one should also develop the habit of a second type of reflection, which occurs less reflexively. After the action is over, it is important to take a few minutes, without the pressure of the immediacy in the situation, to reflect upon what went well and what didn't, and why. In other words, you are reflecting upon what you can learn from your experience to shape future actions. Without this kind of reflection, the lawyer will not improve, but will be stuck in a cycle of repetitive actions. She will be unable to respond to new situations in adaptive ways, and her professional practice will become mechanical, which impedes the nuanced and particular action required. A lawyer who has not developed the habit of reflection will not be able to move back and forth between the general and particular that is necessary to the exercise of practical wisdom.

With these two kinds of reflections, a law student or lawyer will be continually adjusting his or her actions as each situation demands, both in the situation and then in reflecting upon it afterwards so that the next similar situation is informed by both kinds of reflection. This dual reflection process has been described as one of trial and error, reassessment, and then trial again, by which one becomes better and better at what they do. It creates the environment in which the lawyer can continue to develop professional virtues and the personal characteristics that support them, as well as the ability to access them in the right way to do the right thing in a given situation.

Our understanding of the importance of these two kinds of reflection is reinforced by research into how people think (Kahneman 2011). Scientists have found that people often engage two processes at once in reasoning and acting. One process is a shorthand way of thinking, sometimes described as intuition, which allows us to draw upon past patterns and to make quick judgments based on our experiences. Everyone engages in this kind of "thinking fast," and the human ability to do so is a strength that allows us to move through the world efficiently and effectively. Thinking fast means that when you walk in to a courtroom, you know that the judge is the person in the black robe sitting behind the bench. You don't stop and think through your conclusion; rather, you benefit from the ability to form a quick judgment based on your knowledge of the role of judges and your past experiences. A more complex example is that of facial recognition; when you greet a friend, you are not consciously thinking through all of the various features that make you conclude that the person in front of you is indeed someone you know. Your brain processes a great deal of information in a very short time to allow you to call your friend's name confidently and correctly.

But there are times when reliance only upon this process of thinking fast can lead us astray. The wisest people also engage in what has been described as "thinking slow," that is, more contemplative thinking in which they question their intuition and reason anew. Thinking slow acts as a check against being too quick to act based on similarities between situations without paying attention to the nuances or particularities of a new situation. This second type of thinking can help one discern whether reasoning from past patterns is helpful or dangerous: do past patterns help us anticipate and respond appropriately to new, similar situations or do they get in the way of paying attention to the present? Without the check of thinking slow, one may, for example, engage in harmful stereotypes rather than responding to each person as an individual. More generally, one will neglect the need to be attentive to the particulars of the current situation that allow for adaptation.

As we have said, all humans engage in intuitive thinking, or thinking fast. Studies have shown, however, that professionals develop a special kind of professional intuition that, like practical wisdom, may be described as professional expertise. They do so through the accumulation of many experiences. The novice professional will not possess professional intuition. As experience accumulates, the ability of a professional to rely on professional intuition increases. But, as expertise increases, so does the importance of checking that intuition with reflection because the temptation to rely only on intuition increases as well. Even experts have a limit to their expertise; it is the habit of reflection that allows the skilled expert to reliably use intuition by checking it with reflective judgment.

One writer on practical wisdom has captured this combination very well: "[p]ractice builds intuition; reflection on practice builds judgment" (Cahalan 2016, 13). Therefore, the practically wise lawyer will engage in both thinking fast and thinking slow, in reflection while acting and reflection after action. Practical wisdom will moderate and balance the combination so that there is not too much or too little of one or the other. Practical wisdom is what allows just the right amount of each for the particular situation and, hence, the right action.

The habit of learning from others: mentors and role models

In addition to gaining practical wisdom through your own experiences of trial and error, you acquire practical wisdom by learning from others. Because you are a member of a profession, you have a ready-made community of people from whom you can learn. While in law school, that community includes your professors and your peers. The faculty has created situations from which you can gain some of the right kinds of experiences to develop practical wisdom. After graduation, and perhaps before, your professional community will expand to include lawyers with whom you are working or whom you are able to observe.

As with the accumulation of experience, just being a member of a community won't automatically cultivate practical wisdom. Learning from others requires that you take advantage of the opportunities provided. In fact, it is often said that practical wisdom cannot be taught, but that it can be learned. That means that there are many situations that create the opportunity for you to acquire practical wisdom, but it won't happen unless you take advantage of them. Being around good lawyers is essential for the development of practical wisdom, but not sufficient. It is up to you to approach the community of professionals you have joined with an attitude of intentionality; use every opportunity to accumulate the right kinds of experience to gain practical wisdom.

Two ways in which others can help you develop practical wisdom is through mentors and role models. Mentors will help you gain practical wisdom through specific feedback and/or creating situations from which you can gain the valuable experience needed. Think of a mentor as your partner in learning. Mentors allow you to practice alongside them in situations that provide the necessary patterns to develop expertise. Mentors provide feedback that allow you to make corrections to get better at what you are doing.

You are already learning from mentors, even if you are not specifically learning about practical wisdom. For example, when you were a complete novice in the law, a beginning law student, you did not know how to read a judicial opinion, how to do such things as parsing procedural from substantive language, identifying relevant versus irrelevant facts, and understanding the differences between the majority and concurring or dissenting opinions. Nor did you know how to sort cases into meaningful substantive categories, such as recognizing a problem as being one of tort, contracts, or property. By the end of the first year of law school, however, the skills of reading cases and sorting problems by areas of law have become automatic. They are deployed efficiently by the advancing student so that reading and understanding a new case no longer causes the anxiety nor takes the time that it once did. That transition occurs because the law student is repeatedly asked to identify patterns in the cases they are assigned and to reason from both similarities and dissimilarities to understand how the law develops and how it might be applied in future cases.

Learning to read a judicial opinion is a simple example of a novice learning a complex skill from mentors, in this case faculty members, who both create the situation for practice and provide feedback that informs the repeated practice. Students learn from the dialogue with the faculty member, both when they are the one in dialogue and when they are observing their fellow students on the hot seat. They also learn from observing the mentor and taking note of what she finds important in cases and the way that she frames questions and responses.

Note that failure is as important to learning as is success. Mistakes, which are inevitable for the beginner, create opportunities to think about other ways of approaching a problem and to be creative in trying those out. If you were called on in class during your first semester and got something wrong in the way you had read a case, it might have felt like failure and disheartened you. But you should embrace the opportunity to try your new skills, even if you fail at first, because the support and guidance of a good mentor will turn that "failure" into progress. Novices are very much dependent upon the expertise of others, and mentors provide the needed expertise, including correcting mistakes. Mentors explain the process behind their own expertise and guide the development of your skills.

The early stages of learning practical wisdom follow a similar path. Mentors can guide you through new situations and model how to bring to bear all of the personal and professional values that matter. They can provide feedback on your early attempts to exercise practical wisdom and set you up to try again. In law school, you will find such mentorship particularly in simulation courses and in clinical or other experiential learning settings.

Another way in which you can learn from others is through careful observation of role models or exemplars. Be attuned to what the best lawyers do. Seek them out. It may be that you are exposed to lawyers through externship and clinical placements or work experiences while in law school. If you see a lawyer who performs an excellent cross-examination, for example, or a compelling argument to a jury, take the time to learn by identifying what skills the lawyer called upon; how did she react to the witness's answer or to the facial expressions and demeanor of the jurors? Could you detect moments when the lawyer used reflection to reshape the action? How did the lawyer balance the lawyerly virtues?

Exemplars are living examples of people with high levels of skill and expertise. They can be someone close to you, or they can be someone whom you have never met, but whom you have read about. When you engage with an exemplar, you can begin to compare and contrast yourself and begin to imagine yourself in the role or situation of that person. An exemplar provides you with a model. You may at first mimic what the exemplar does, for example, framing your closing argument in the same way or moving about the courtroom as the exemplar does. As time goes on, you will begin to adapt the lessons learned to your own style. In that way, learning from exemplars is an important step in the development of your own professional identity. Just as with learning from mentors, learning from exemplars requires that you seek out the opportunities provided and be attentive to using them to help you gain the right kind of experience.

Learning from exemplars is useful generally but is particularly important to the development of practical wisdom. You can read about lawyers who made difficult decisions in complex and uncertain situations. If you are fortunate, you will have the chance to observe an experienced practitioner exercise practical wisdom and have the opportunity to talk about the process and how the ultimate decision or advice was the right balance among competing concerns in that particular situation. Exemplars, in print or in person, can give you a clear picture of what the exercise of practical wisdom looks like and give you a sort of mental template to use when your time comes.

CONCLUSION

Practical wisdom is the sixth of the six lawyerly virtues. It is the master virtue that allows you to effectively deploy all of your personal and professional virtues and skills in a complex moment of professional practice. As the master virtue, it may take the longest for you to acquire; indeed, it requires a lifelong process of development. Practical wisdom is dependent upon your acquiring the other five virtues and the continued development of personal characteristics such as kindness, courage, empathy, and integrity. You must be intentional about forming the right habits so that you can reflexively call upon your professional expertise and adapt to changing and uncertain situations. You must be aware of what kinds of experiences will support your development of practical wisdom and of those that will impede it. The effort will be worth it, however, because practical wisdom allows you to best exercise your full identity as a lawyer.

Practical wisdom, by allowing you to fully live out your professional identity, not only supports your being an ethical and effective lawyer, but it also supports your living a life of well-being and satisfaction. Aristotle called it "flourishing," and argued that practical wisdom is necessary for human happiness. And, once again, modern research supports Aristotle. As we saw in Chapter 2, scientists who study human well-being and happiness have repeatedly found that those who are engaged with meaningful work are those who report the highest levels of well-being and satisfaction. In other words, the characteristics that produce practical wisdom are the same ones that produce happiness.

DISCUSSION QUESTIONS AND PROBLEMS

Note: Because practical wisdom is the most complex of the six virtues, several of the problems for this chapter are also more complex.

1   Implementing practical wisdom as a lawyer will not be the first time that you have had to resolve multiple goals and competing demands in situations of inherent uncertainty. You have no doubt done so in your pre-law school life or as a law student. Think of a time when a friend or family member asked for your help in solving a difficult situation, or when you asked a friend or family member for help in such a situation. Recall with as much detail as you can the things that you talked about—what were the goals of appropriately resolving the dilemma; what alternatives did you discuss; and why was the particular resolution reached? How was the decision ultimately implemented, and why? Can you identify any of the six virtues (or their analogs) that were at work? For example, was there concern about friendship or familial relationships, comparable to the lawyerly virtue of fidelity to the client? Were there rules that

mattered, comparable to the lawyerly virtue of fidelity to the law? Was there a concern about politeness or respect (similar to civility), or using skills well (competence), or the effect on others (public spiritedness)? Write an essay in which you describe how the experience will be helpful to your cultivating practical wisdom as a lawyer.

2   Arrange an informal interview with a lawyer you know or someone recommended by your law school's faculty or staff. Ask the lawyer about times when he or she has had to call on professional judgment in difficult situations of competing tensions and uncertain outcomes. Ask them to identify what their goals were, how they went about making a decision about the right thing to do, what was difficult about implementing that decision, and what they learned from the situation. Ask them about how their professional judgment has grown over time and what advice they can offer a new lawyer about the best ways to learn from others and to learn from experience.

3   Practice implementing practical wisdom in the following situation: You are an attorney who represents a defendant in a personal injury case that arises from an automobile accident. Your client was driving one of the cars involved in the accident, and he is being sued by a passenger in his car. You became the lawyer in the case because your client is insured, and the insurance contract provides that the insurance company will hire and pay a lawyer if he is sued. You are regularly hired by this insurance company to represent its insureds in such cases. In fact, such work from this insurance company represents approximately 40% of your yearly billings. The policy limits are $250,000, and the insurance company has the power to approve or reject any settlement within the policy limits. Any judgment or settlement in excess of $250,000 will have to be paid personally by your client.

   The plaintiff is an 18-year-old man who seeks damages for a bruised sternum that he allegedly suffered as a result of the accident. You are entitled under the rules of civil procedure to have the plaintiff examined by a doctor of your choosing, which you have done. The doctor confirms that the plaintiff has a bruised sternum. Based upon your experience and prior cases, a reasonable estimate of the plaintiff's damages for a bruised sternum would be $15,000. To your surprise, however, the doctor also tells you that the plaintiff has an aortic aneurysm that may or may not have resulted from the accident. There is no way to be sure whether the aneurysm was a preexisting condition, although you suspect that a jury likely would find that it was not preexisting but rather was caused by the accident. Based upon your experience and prior cases, a reasonable estimate of the plaintiff's damages for an aortic aneurysm would be $400,000.

   You estimate that it will be approximately two years before the case could come to trial. The aneurysm is life threatening but has no current symptoms. It could rupture at any time, although the odds of it rupturing on any particular day are infinitesimal. It might never rupture. If it did rupture, however, death would almost inevitably follow quickly. The problem is remediable with surgery, which would cost the plaintiff $15,000 out of pocket (his health insurance would cover the rest of the cost). As far as you can tell, the plaintiff and his lawyer have no idea about the aneurysm. The plaintiff's lawyer has the absolute right to receive your doctor's report if the lawyer requests it, but he has not done so. Otherwise, you have no obligation under the rules of civil procedure to deliver your doctor's report.

   Under the rules of professional conduct that apply to you, the information you have about the aortic aneurysm is confidential. You may reveal it to others (besides to the client and the insurance company) only: (1) if you obtain informed consent of the client or (2) if you reasonably believe that disclosure is reasonably necessary to prevent death or substantial bodily harm. The rules of professional conduct place no obligation on you to reveal the information to the plaintiff. Your obligations under the rules of professional conduct to communicate with your client include the following: You must (1) reasonably consult with the client about the means by which the client's objectives are to be accomplished; (2) keep the client reasonably informed about the status of the matter; (3) explain a matter to the extent reasonably necessary to permit the client to make informed decisions regarding the representation. By custom and by contract, you are authorized to reveal this information to the insurance company, even though it is not your client. Your routine is to advise the insurance adjuster of any important developments in a case that you are handling for its policyholders.

Write a short essay in which you explain what you will do and why. Remember that your goal is to do the "right" thing, in the "right" way, for the "right" reasons. Multiple virtues are in play, and they may be in tension with each other. You must decide what to do, and how to do it, under conditions of irreducible uncertainty. As you resolve the problem, identify what your goals are and which virtues are implicated. Describe how you will ensure that you are using the right amount of each virtue for this particular situation. Once you have decided what to do, you must also decide how you are going to implement your decision. For example, if you decide to reveal the information you have learned about the plaintiff, discuss how you will do that in as much detail as you can. If you decide not to reveal the aneurysm, discuss what that means for your next steps in representing your client, and discuss those in as much detail as you can. Then read the case upon which this problem is based, *Spaulding v. Zimmerman*, 116 N.W. 2d 704 (Minnesota 1962).

4   Practice implementing practical wisdom in the following situation: You represent a client who is a successful businessperson and is beginning a new business of manufacturing and selling baseball bats made of bamboo. She believes that the market for wooden baseball bats is going to increase for several reasons: growing safety concerns about metal bats; the greater durability of wooden bats; and environmental benefits to making the bats of a sustainable resource. With your help, the client has been in protracted negotiations with her brother, who operates an import-export business, to supply the wood for the bats. The contract calls for the brother to supply all of the wood that your client will need for the next five years at a set price. One of the sticking points in negotiations has been the brother's desire for the contract to include an escape clause, which would excuse the brother's performance in the case of "political unrest" in the country of origin. Your client has finally conceded to including the escape clause in the contract, although unhappily. Now that negotiations are concluded, the brother's lawyer has prepared the final draft of the contract, obtained the brother's signature on it, and sent it to you for your client's signature. As you are reviewing the contract in preparation for having your client and sign it, you realize that the lawyer has omitted the much-discussed escape clause.

Write a short essay in which you explain what you will do and why. Assume that the rules of conduct permit you to reveal the omission to the brother's lawyer without telling your client about it. Remember that your goal is to do the "right" thing, in the "right" way, for the "right" reasons. Multiple virtues are in play, and they may be in tension with each other. You must decide what to do, and how to do it, under conditions of irreducible uncertainty. As you resolve the problem, identify what your goals are and which virtues are implicated. Describe how you will ensure that you are using the right amount of each virtue for this particular situation. Once you have decided what to do, you must also decide how you are going to implement your decision. For example, if you decide to reveal the mistake to the other lawyer, do you talk to your client before doing so? If so, what are the tone and content of that conversation? What if she instructs you not to reveal the mistake and wants to sign the contract as it is? If you decide to advise your client to sign the contract without revealing the mistake, what do you do about advising her about any potential consequences of that decision?

5   Practice implementing practical wisdom in the following situation: You are a junior partner in a branch office of a large law firm. You have become concerned about your mentor in the firm, who is also the managing partner of the branch office in which you work. You and he work together on matters for a significant client of the firm, a Fortune 500 company. In fact, over half of your billable hours each year come from work on behalf of that client. In going over billing records, you discover that your mentor has been billing large amounts of time to the client that you are reasonably confident he could not have actually performed. In particular, he has recorded spending time in several meetings with you that you know did not actually occur. What do you do? What considerations will you take into account in deciding a course of action, including your personal relationship with your mentor, your duty to the client, your position in the firm, and perhaps others? What virtues are at work in this situation? Do you perceive tension among the virtues? How will using practical wisdom help you decide what to do and how to go about doing it?

REFERENCE LIST AND SUGGESTED READINGS

American Bar Association Standing Committee on Professionalism. 2013. *Essential Qualities of the Professional Lawyer*, ed. Paul A. Haskins. Chicago: ABA Publishing.

Cahalan, Kathleen. 2016. Integrative Knowing and Practical Wisdom. *Reflective Practice: Formation and Supervision in Ministry* 36:7.

Floyd, Daisy Hurst. 2012. Pedagogy and Purpose: Teaching for Practical Wisdom. *Mercer Law Review* 63:943.

Floyd, Daisy Hurst. 2012. Practical Wisdom: Reimagining Legal Education. *University of St. Thomas Law Journal* 10:195.

Floyd, Daisy Hurst, and Timothy W. Floyd. 2016. Professional Identity and Formation. *Learning from Practice: A Text for Experiential Legal Education*, ed. Leah Wortham, Alexander Scherr, Nancy Maurer, and Susan L. Brooks. St. Paul: West Academic Publishing.

Floyd, Timothy W., and John Gallagher. 2007. Legal Ethics, Narrative, and Professional Identity: The Story of David Spaulding. *Mercer Law Review* 59: 941.

Mercer University. 2013. *Toward Human Flourishing: Character, Practical Wisdom, and Professional Formation*, ed. Mark L. Jones, Paul A. Lewis, and Kelly E. Reffitt. Macon: Mercer University Press.

Kahneman, Daniel. 2011. *Thinking, Fast and Slow*. New York: Farrar, Straus and Giroux.

May, William F. 2001. *Beleaguered Rulers: The Public Obligation of the Professional*. Louisville: Westminster John Knox Press.

Schon, Donald A. 1987. *Educating the Reflective Practitioner*. San Francisco: Jossey-Bass.

Schwartz, Barry, and Kenneth Sharpe. 2010. *Practical Wisdom: The Right Way to Do the Right Thing*. New York: Riverhead Books.

Sullivan, William M. 2005. *Work and Integrity: The Crisis and Promise of Professionalism in America*. San Francisco: Jossey-Bass.

Sullivan, William M., Anne Colby, Judith Welch Wegner, Lloyd Bond, and Lee S. Shulman. 2007. *Educating Lawyers: Preparation for the Profession of Law*. San Francisco: Jossey-Bass.

Sullivan, William M., and Matthew Rosin. 2008. *A New Agenda for Higher Education: Life of the Mind for Practice*. San Francisco: Jossey-Bass.

9

PROFESSIONAL IDENTITY AND THE FUTURE OF THE LEGAL PROFESSION

INTRODUCTION

The legal profession that you will soon be entering is in the midst of rapid change. That is no secret. The American Bar Association recently completed a two-year study on the future of legal services. Books with alarming titles that include *The Vanishing American Lawyer*, *The American Legal Profession in Crisis*, and *The End of Lawyers* have received widespread, and justified, attention. Many lawyers in practice today entered the profession before lawyers were using email and voicemail, to say nothing of personal computers, smart phones, and the internet. They could not have foreseen those developments. The practice of law changed under their feet, just as it will under yours. It is a fair question to ask how the "traditional" values of the legal profession, which we have urged you to incorporate into your sense of self as a lawyer, relate to the profession you are joining.

Let us begin by urging you to take the long view. These are turbulent times, and with turbulence comes anxiety. But remember that people have been using the philosophy of virtue ethics to strive for excellence and fulfillment for well over 2,000 years. And lawyers for centuries have been contributing their distinctive skills and judgment to improve the lives of their clients and their communities. History also offers us some examples of well-known lawyers who helped navigate change and meet threats to the well-being of the world. A lawyer drafted the Declaration of Independence. Lawyers wrote the United States Constitution. A lawyer guided us through the Civil War and signed the Emancipation Proclamation. In addition to those well-known examples, countless numbers of lawyers have helped clients through the joys and crises of their daily lives in significant ways, regardless of changes in forms of government, technology, or social institutions, and found deep meaning and satisfaction in their work. Dallas lawyer John McShane stated it well when he said,

> *I want lawyers to know that it is not only possible to have a joyful, meaningful law practice, but that there isn't another activity around that offers more opportunity for both personal growth and making a difference in other people's lives.*
>
> *(Keeva 2000)*

It would be foolhardy of us to try to predict with a pretense of certainty how the legal profession will change in your lifetime. But there are enough discernible trends today to warrant a discussion of how the right kind of professional identity, as we have defined it, will still matter in the decades to come. Many of the opportunities and challenges arise from the rapid evolution of technology. Others relate to globalization. And regardless of these trends, there will be continuing needs for lawyers to protect the rule of law and an enduring role for practical wisdom and the other five virtues that should comprise your professional identity.

TECHNOLOGY

Using technology to help and protect your clients

Innovations in technology are driving much of the change in the legal profession. The comments to Model Rule of Professional Conduct 1.1, on competence, were recently amended to state that "a lawyer should keep abreast of changes in the law and its practice, including the benefits and risks associated with relevant technology…." A lawyer's use of technology has enormous potential to benefit a client. You can investigate jurors with a click on a Google search rather than the use of a private investigator. You can access almost every case that has ever been decided from your phone, without the necessity of maintaining the expensive overhead of a law library. You can check the subsequent history of a case within seconds online rather than in minutes with books. You can save hundreds of hours, and save your clients thousands of dollars, by using technology assisted review of voluminous documents in discovery. And so on. Competence and fidelity to your client demand that you keep up to date and use emerging technology when it benefits the client.

Your duty of competence with respect to technology also includes knowledge of risks, especially with respect to the protection of confidential client information. We live in an era of growing dangers from efforts to obtain unauthorized access to private data. In 2016, a Russian hacker gained access to the computer network of the Wall Street law firm Cravath, Swain & Moore. In 2017, a large offshore law firm headquartered in Bermuda suffered a breach that exposed more than 13 million files. A lawyer who does not understand and employ basic safeguards against such efforts is not acting with competence. The means of fulfilling the duty to protect client information will have to evolve as quickly as the schemes for gaining unauthorized access to it.

Technology and the delivery of legal services

Competence is not the only virtue implicated by changing technology. Some of the greatest challenges for the traditional values of the legal profession relate to the duty to practice in a spirit of public service. Remember that one of the requirements for doing so is regulation of the profession for the benefit of the public and not for the benefit of lawyers. Changes in the ways that legal services can be delivered have the potential to threaten segments of the legal profession and at the same time greatly benefit the public. The challenge is for lawyers to deal with those changes with the public interest, rather than their private interests, in mind.

These issues center around new kinds of Legal Service Providers (LSPs). The ABA Commission on the Future of Legal Services divided new LSPs into two kinds. The first is a "regulated" LSP, a non-lawyer who is officially authorized to provide legal services within certain limitations.

As you saw in Chapter 6, a state might choose to permit "legal technicians" to render certain limited legal services. The second type of new LSP is the one with which we are concerned here. These are the "unregulated" LSP's that provide legal assistance via an online platform. The best-known examples are LegalZoom and Rocket Lawyer. A customer can go online and create legal documents such as wills and contracts by answering a series of questions. The customer's answers automatically determine the next question in a series of "branches" or "decision trees." Eventually, once all the relevant questions have been answered, the document will be printed and sent for execution in exchange for payment of a flat fee. If you have ever used TurboTax or a similar product for doing your taxes, then you are familiar with the process. These unregulated LSPs are popular and successful and have thus far warded off efforts to shut them down for engaging in the unauthorized practice of law.

The fees charged by web sites like LegalZoom and Rocket Lawyer are substantially below what most attorneys would charge for the same service. We offer no opinion on the quality of its final product, but LegalZoom, and other web sites like it, undoubtedly are making certain legal services more readily available at cheaper cost. Some customers probably would have proceeded without a lawyer if this type of cheap online product were not available. But some of the customers would have paid a lawyer to create the will or the contract and instead chose the easier and cheaper option. To the extent that these unregulated LSPs are serving customers who otherwise would have become some lawyer's client, they are threats to lawyers who make their bread-and-butter living from such services and, if you become one of those lawyers, may test your commitment to practicing in a spirit of public service.

Tomorrow, or next month, or next year, there will be further innovations in the legal services market. New LSPs will emerge. Those innovations may reach clients who would never have sought a lawyer, or they may divert clients from lawyers to new and cheaper ways of obtaining services. Whether and how to regulate these innovations will be questions, at least initially, for the legal profession itself. This is where your duty to practice in a spirit of public service comes in. Some of these innovations may pose a threat to the public because they are of such inferior quality. To protect the public – not yourself – you should step forward as a member of a self-regulating profession and do what is necessary. Other innovations, perhaps already including online document creation services, may benefit the public but hurt your bottom line. Your duty then will be just as clear but harder: get out of the way.

The ABA provided excellent guidance and encouragement for this endeavor when in 2016 it adopted its Model Regulatory Objectives, which capture the challenge for you as a member of the legal profession in times of such change. The objectives should remind you that practicing in a spirit of public service will require you to keep in mind, among other objectives, "protection of the public," "meaningful access to justice and information about the law," and "delivery of affordable and accessible legal services" (American Bar Association 2016, 1). We do not mean to minimize how hard it may be to stand aside and allow LSPs to thrive at your expense, but your duties as a lawyer require you put the public interest first.

Technology and new risks of incivility

Changes in how lawyers practice already have presented new challenges for civility, and we predict more will come.

Recall that one of the key components of civility is courtesy. Technology has changed law practice dramatically with respect to the ways in which lawyers interact with each other. Today lawyers routinely communicate by email and text messages. The ease and rapidity of these methods of communication makes them efficient, but there is a downside. Before, without the ability instantaneously to leave asynchronous electronic messages, lawyers interacted by mail or through personal conversations, either face-to-face or by telephone. They had the time to reflect upon and consider carefully what they wrote or said. Although there was incivility among lawyers even then, it was at least somewhat constrained by the slower pace of communication and the direct nature of conversations.

New methods of communication increase the likelihood of discourteous, uncivil communication between lawyers because they can happen so quickly, before lawyers have the time to reflect, and because they are indirect. Yet the dangers of incivility, in terms of increased cost and acrimony in resolving disputes or doing deals, are still present. You saw in Chapter 7 some examples of incivility in the use of voicemail and email. Whatever new methods of communication the future brings, you will need to be on guard to resist new temptations to be discourteous brought about by fast and indirect means of communication. Your duty of civility demands it.

GLOBALIZATION

Technology is not the only force driving change in the legal profession. There is also a trend toward globalization of the practice, particularly as it relates to the representation of businesses.

The most significant challenge from globalization if you enter this type of practice is likely to be your fidelity to the client. The form of organization in which you find yourself practicing may be different than anything you would see in the United States today, where lawyers practice alone or in partnership or association in law firms owned and controlled only by lawyers. Model Rule 5.4 prohibits lawyers from practicing law in a partnership with any non-lawyer. Among other things, this rule prohibits most Multi-Disciplinary Practices (MDPs), through which legal services and non-legal services (such as accounting) are delivered by the same firm. Rule 5.4 also forbids almost all arrangements in which a non-lawyer owns any part of a for-profit professional corporation or association authorized to practice law, and it prohibits lawyers from practicing in such a firm if a non-lawyer is a corporate officer or director of the organization. The purpose of these restrictions is to protect one aspect of the lawyer's duty of fidelity to the client, the duty to render independent professional advice free from the pressures that non-lawyer ownership or participation might bring. You can view Rule 5.4 as a prophylactic measure to ensure fidelity to the client by forbidding certain business arrangements that might cause a lawyer not to put the clients' interests first.

It is highly likely that this will change. In the future, the practice of law in the United States probably will permit a lawyer to practice in so-called Alternative Business Structures (ABS). The ABA Commission on the Future of Legal Services studied whether the rules of conduct should be amended to grant such permission (American Bar Association Commission on the Future of Legal Services 2016). The commission defined ABS to include some combination of non-lawyer ownership in law firms, including passive investment, and the operation of the ABS as an MDP, in which it would provide legal services in addition to non-legal services. Although the commission's report stopped short of an unalloyed endorsement of ABS, it did recommend further study of the concept and the gathering of data in jurisdictions that choose to allow them. As of this writing, only two American jurisdictions permit any form of ABS.

Despite the timid recommendations of the ABA Commission, it appears clear to us that you will be permitted to practice in an ABS in the not-so-distant future. The primary reason is global competition. Many foreign jurisdictions already permit lawyers to practice in organizations that have non-lawyer ownership and provide legal and non-legal services. Large U.S. law firms now compete in a global marketplace, and the current restrictions of our rules of conduct place those firms at a disadvantage. Their cost of capital is greater because they cannot rely on non-lawyer investment. Their ability to be "one-stop shops" by the provision of non-legal services makes them less competitive globally. For these reasons, we believe that permission to practice in the United States in an ABS will come sooner rather than later.

If we are right, then those among you who practice in an ABS will face new pressures on your fidelity to your clients. Remember that your duty includes putting the interests of your client above the interests of others, including yourself and your firm. Sometimes the independent advice that flows from this duty might mean that the client pays your firm less money, maybe because you counsel the client to settle a dispute without litigation or to back out of a large business deal. Such advice might be displeasing to your firm's investors or to your non-lawyer partners because it costs the firm money, yet giving the advice remains your duty nevertheless. Lawyers of previous generations have been insulated from these pressures because of the prohibitions on non-lawyer investment and MDPs. You may not be, and you will have to fall back upon your sense of self as a lawyer and resist the temptation not to put the clients' interests first.

PRESERVING THE RULE OF LAW

Part of your duty of fidelity to the law is to protect the law. You do that mostly day-to-day by counseling clients not to break the law, by refusing to help them do so, and by making sure that you abide by the law when you advocate for clients. But this duty can intersect with your broader responsibility to practice in a spirit of public service, and it will call upon you to do more when the times demand it.

There certainly have been times when lawyers were needed to stand up for the rule of law. In the wake of Brown v. Board of Education, 347 U.S. 483 (1954), politicians throughout the south decried the legitimacy of the courts, sought to strip jurisdiction from the federal courts over civil rights claims, and even sought to impeach judges because they disliked the decisions. Lawyers like Thurgood Marshall, Horace Ward, Constance Baker Motley, and Donald Hollowell stood up and with great courage helped to preserve the rule of law in a trying time. In case after case across the country, it was lawyers who ensured that the lofty pronouncements of Brown were translated into reality in desegregated classrooms.

In the 1970's, the Watergate scandal brought us to the brink of a Constitutional crisis. The President of the United States obstructed an investigation into the illegal activities of people associated with his campaign. He may have destroyed evidence when an infamous 17-minute gap appeared in one of the recordings of his conversations. He fired the special prosecutor who had been appointed to investigate the scandal. It took courageous lawyers to ensure that our system of government survived. Archibald Cox, Elliot Richardson, William Ruckelshaus, Leon Jaworski, and many others acted with extraordinary fidelity to the law when the times demanded it. Attorneys General Edward Levi and Griffin Bell worked diligently after the fact to repair the damage. The rule of law survived.

There are numerous other examples. Such fundamental challenges to the rule of law ebb and flow, but history teaches us not to be complacent. Your generation's time to stand up will come, if it is not already here. No technology can take the place of lawyers at such a time. It will only be the deployment of the virtue of fidelity to the law by lawyers like you that the rule of law will be preserved.

THE ENDURING ROLES OF PRACTICAL WISDOM AND PROFESSIONAL IDENTITY

As you saw in Chapter 8, the first five virtues are manifested through practical wisdom, the master virtue that enables you to form judgments about what you should do, or what advice you should give, especially when you or your client may have multiple goals that are in tension with each other under conditions of uncertainty. Practical wisdom is a service tailored to the particular situation. In the terms used by Richard Susskind, a leading voice on the future of the legal profession, it is a "bespoke" service, one that is necessary when the "client's circumstances are unique and ... requires the handcrafting or fashioning of a solution, honed specifically for the individual matter at issue" (Susskind 2013, 24). Lawyers have been offering this bespoke service for many centuries, and a crucial question for the future of the profession is to what extent a need for "bespoke" service will survive.

Many of the predictions about the future of the legal profession concern work that, in Susskind's terms, is not "bespoke" but rather is "standardized," "systemized," "packaged," or "commoditized." To see the distinction among these concepts, imagine a lawyer who is asked to create a contract for a client. The lawyer's work is *standardized* when the lawyer uses a preexisting form or template as a starting point for a client's work. That would almost always be the case. It is *systematized* when the lawyer uses computerized checklists or fill-in-the-blank decision trees to "assemble" a final document such as a contract for a client. For more routine types of contracts, such a system saves time and minimizes errors. The contract could be the result of *packaging* if the lawyer made the contract-drafting system available for the client to use to create the document without the personal involvement of the lawyer. In the extreme, a contract may be so simple that it can be *commoditized* by making the form freely available on the web, perhaps as a "loss leader" for a firm that seeks to generate clients by giving away some simple services.

Practical wisdom will still be necessary for work that is standardized. The "form" – or more generally the lawyer's internal template for handling a particular kind of problem – still must be adapted to the particular circumstances presented by the client. That process will require the lawyer to weigh a variety of factors in order to make a judgment. Practical wisdom will also be required in the initial creation of the legal product that eventually is systematized, packaged or commoditized. Some lawyer, at some point, must have made a judgment about how to construct the decision tree that is built into a systematized or packaged product. But once the legal service is actually systematized, packaged or commoditized, there is no more room for practical wisdom.

No one doubts, however, that there will still be situations that require a "bespoke" service that includes practical wisdom and the other five virtues. High-stakes litigation is the prime example. Lawyers who are helping corporate clients navigate a "bet the company" case will need to cultivate and deploy their practical wisdom. Clients in personal plight cases such as divorce, personal injury, consumer bankruptcy, criminal defense, and the like, will also need bespoke services. These individuals, unlike executives in large corporations and their in house counsel, usually have little previous experience in the legal system, and therefore need lawyers to communicate clearly and effectively what their legal rights and options are. The problems in these matters are often fraught with interpersonal complexity and emotional discord. Communication skills, empathy, emotional intelligence, and practical wisdom are especially important for lawyers in these cases. Not everything can be systematized, packaged or commoditized.

Some speculate whether technology could someday take the place of lawyers. If IBM's Watson can win Jeopardy, then why could it not process all the relevant variables and spit out some practical wisdom, perhaps through your smart speaker, in the voice of Alexa or Siri? Never say never, but right now even the proponents of the use of artificial intelligence in the law do not believe that it can handle uncertainty and reason across a broad range of conflicting objectives as well as a wise lawyer can. And clients who need compassionate communication and guidance will not get it from artificial intelligence and a smart speaker. The robots are not ready to take over yet.

Technology will, however, play an important role in the exercise of your practical wisdom and other duties to your clients. To make the right judgment or to give the right advice, you may need the best information you can get about any number of variables. Traditionally, lawyers have relied upon their personal experience to inform their judgments. Although we have not tested and thus cannot warrant the efficacy of the products, there are vendors who claim to be able to use technology to generate better information than you could generate in more traditional ways. ROSS is a legal research platform whose owners claim that, through the use of artificial intelligence, ROSS can more efficiently search relevant case law. Lex Machina is a technology that takes raw litigation data and use algorithms (as well as humans) to predict how a specific judge will respond to a particular motion, or to learn about opposing counsel's experience, or to learn about an opposing party's experience before a particular court. Undoubtedly, there are other vendors who make similar claims for their products.

For purposes of your professional identity, however, the important thing to realize is these tools *assist* you in the exercise of practical wisdom and the deployment of the other virtues of the professional lawyer, but they do not *displace* you. Relevant information is essential to good lawyering, and more relevant information is better, but knowledge is not the same as wisdom. Good lawyers will still need to deploy the master virtue of practical wisdom and the other virtues in service to their clients.

CONCLUSION

We began this book by urging you to learn about the traditional values of the legal profession and resolve to make those values part of your sense of self as a lawyer. We made the case that you will be a better and a happier lawyer if you will do that. We have tried to help you understand those values deeply and to offer suggestions about how to live up to them when they are challenged. You are entering the legal profession at a time of dramatic changes and might rightly wonder what those "traditional" values will mean to you in your time at the bar. No one really knows. But we are convinced, and we hope you are too, that internalizing the six virtues of the professional lawyer will continue to be essential as you strive to make your work meaningful for others and meaningful to you. Competence, fidelity to the client, fidelity to law, public spiritedness, civility, and practical wisdom—these are the virtues you need, even in the midst of change, and we wish you well as you strive to acquire and deploy them in the world that waits for you.

DISCUSSION QUESTIONS AND PROBLEMS

1   Reflect upon the type of practice you wish to have. What technology do you anticipate using to help you practice better and more efficiently? Do you foresee any risks to your practice from technology and, if so, how would you minimize them? Do you have any fear that the type of practice you wish to have could be affected by the availability of legal technicians, online document creation services like LegalZoom, or other technologies? How does that prospect affect your plans for using your law degree?

2   When you are a lawyer, you will have many choices about how to communicate with opposing counsel and clients. There is regular mail, telephone, email, text messaging, social media, and presumably other choices. Suppose you are in charge of your own firm. Write a memo to a new associate who is going to work for you about when to use each means of communication. Include some rules of etiquette about what you expect in communications in each medium.

3   Make an inventory of your technological skills. Reflect upon how you can use those skills to market yourself to older lawyers who may be eager to employ a new lawyer who has such skills in addition to the usual skills that you learn in law school.

4   Interview a lawyer who has been in practice for 30 years or more. Ask about how the practice of law has changed and how the lawyer adapted to those changes. Seek advice about how you can be ready to adapt to change as it occurs during your career.

5   Imagine yourself as a partner in a firm that includes both lawyers and accountants as partners, and that the managing partner of the firm is not a lawyer. Now suppose that you learn that one of your lawyer partners made a significant mistake in the representation of a client. Explain to the non-lawyer managing partner why the client needs to be informed of the mistake, even if it means that the client fires the firm and files a malpractice action against it. How would you respond to an instruction not to inform the client?

6   Go online to the web site of an unregulated legal services provider such as LegalZoom. Start the process of creating a last will and testament (you need not use your real name). Stop when you believe that the online platform with which you are interacting has engaged in the "practice of law." Critique your experience with LegalZoom and reflect on whether and how the legal profession should seek to regulate it.

7   Suppose you are an associate at a law firm that defends corporations from product liability suits all over the country. Research the latest high-tech products that are designed to help lawyers like those in your firm give better advice or make better decisions for your clients. Such technologies, for example, might involve using the internet to research the background of potential jurors or promote the use of "big data" analytics to predict how a judge will decide a particular issue. Be prepared to report back on what you find and make recommendations about what new products the firm should investigate further.

REFERENCE LIST AND SUGGESTED READINGS

American Bar Association Commission on the Future of Legal Services. 2016. *Report on the Future of Legal Services in the United States.* www.americanbar.org/content/dam/aba/images/abanews/2016FLS Report_FNL_WEB.pdf.

American Bar Association House of Delegates. 2016. *ABA Model Regulatory Objectives for the Provision of Legal Services.* www.abajournal.com/files/2016_hod_midyear_105.authcheckdam.pdf.

American Bar Association Standing Committee on Professionalism. 2015. *The Relevant Lawyer: Reimagining the Future of the Legal Profession*, ed. Paul A. Haskins. Chicago: American Bar Association Publishing.

Barton, Benjamin H. 2016. *Glass Half Full: The Decline and Rebirth of the Legal Profession*. New York: Oxford University Press.

Barton, Benjamin H., and Stephanos Bibas. 2018. *Rebooting Justice: More Technology, Fewer Lawyers, and the Future of Law*. New York: Encounter Books.

Harper, Stephen J. 2013. *The Lawyer Bubble*. New York: Basic Books.

Keeva, Steven. 2000. Passionate Practitioner. *ABA Journal* 86:56.

Moliterno, James E. 2013. *The American Legal Profession in Crisis*. New York: Oxford University Press.

Morgan, Thomas D. 2016. Inverted Thinking about Law as a Profession or Business. *Journal of the Professional Lawyer* 2016:115.

Morgan, Thomas D. 2010. *The Vanishing American Lawyer*. New York: Oxford University Press.

Susskind, Richard E. 2008. *The End of Lawyers? Rethinking the Nature of Legal Services*. New York: Oxford University Press.

Susskind, Richard E. 2013. *Tomorrow's Lawyers*. Oxford: Oxford University Press.

INDEX